# PWER<sub>TO</sub> SERVE

# P⦿WER TO
# SERVE

## Living a Joyful Spirit-Filled Life

Walter G. Fremont
Carson K. Fremont

AMBASSADOR INTERNATIONAL
GREENVILLE, SOUTH CAROLINA & BELFAST, NORTHERN IRELAND

www.ambassador-international.com

# Power to Serve
## Living a Joyful Spirit-Filled Life.

© 2009 Trudy M. Fremont

Printed in the United States of America

## ISBN 978-1-935507-00-0

Cover Design & Page Layout by David Siglin of A&E Media

**AMBASSADOR INTERNATIONAL**
Emerald House
427 Wade Hampton Blvd.
Greenville, SC 29609, USA
www.ambassador-international.com


**AMBASSADOR PUBLICATIONS**
Providence House
Ardenlee Street
Belfast, BT6 8QJ, Northern Ireland, UK
www.ambassador-productions.com


*The colophon is a trademark of Ambassador*

DEDICATED TO ALL THE SPIRIT-FILLED MEN
AND WOMEN WE HAVE CO-LABORED WITH IN
THE MANY YEARS OF OUR MINISTIES AS A
TEACHER AT BOB JONES UNIVERSITY AND AS A
MISSIONARY ON FOREIGN FIELDS.

# TABLE OF CONTENTS

# TABLES

# FOREWORD

A. W. Tozer, godly Missionary Alliance pastor of a past generation, once observed that "the idea of the Spirit held by the average church member is so vague as to be nearly non-existent." "When he thinks of the matter at all," Tozer continued, "he is likely to try to imagine a nebulous substance like a wisp of invisible smoke which is said to be present in churches and to hover over good people when they are dying."

If Tozer was right, and he probably was, then it is no wonder that the deeply satisfying experience of living a Spirit-filled life is unknown even to many professing Christians. They need enlightening scriptural guidance. Those who sense their need often search for help in local Christian bookstores. But the fantastical books on the Holy Spirit that glut the shelves confuse at best; at worst they mislead. It is apparent that not everyone writing about the Spirit has actually been taught by Him.

Appendix A of this volume recounts the lifelong growth of walking in the Spirit experienced by its authors, Walter and Carson Fremont. It was only at the gentle insistence of friends that their personal testimonies were included at all, and, with characteristic modesty, the Fremonts did so only in an appendix rather than (as many writers would have done) as the main story line of the book. That in itself communicates that the focus of their work is, in all truthfulness, on the blessed Spirit of God rather than on their personal experiences (blessed as they are as well). But at the risk of incurring their disapproval, I would like to suggest that the testimonies be read first. Not only are they informative introductions to the authors themselves, but much more, they are the heartwarming evidence that these two gracious servants of the Lord know personally the Spirit-filled life of which they write.

Most importantly, what the authors know experientially is reassuringly scriptural, and it is to this biblical aspect of the subject that they give preeminence. Beginning with certain fundamentals foundational to Spirit-filled living, they frame up with scores of Scriptures the progressive building of a believer's obedient responses to the Spirit right through from salvation to gifted service. The result for any reader who yields to this biblical development will be a "body" that testifies that it is, indeed, "the temple of the Holy Ghost" (I Corinthians 6:19). If that is what edification is all about—building up believers "for an habitation of God through the Spirit" (Ephesians 2:22)—then this book genuinely edifies. And that, as much as any other of its credentials, is the evidence that the Spirit of God, who commanded expressly, "Let all things be done unto edifying" (I Corinthians 14:26), has indeed guided during the writing of this book.

Mark Minnick
Pastor, Mount Calvary Baptist Church
Greenville, South Carolina

# PREFACE

There is a broad spectrum of beliefs in evangelical circles about the Spirit-filled life. These beliefs vary from the emotional, demonstrative, Pentecostal-Charismatic movement to the staid, contemplative, Keswick-deeper life movement. There is a multitude of differing beliefs between these two extremes. Many new Christians and the majority of church members, when thinking about the Holy Spirit in their life, confused by the different viewpoints, choose to ignore the idea of the Spirit-filled life. They live mediocre Christian lives doing the best they can, hoping that God will understand. Except for their church attendance there is little difference in their lifestyle, their thinking, and their reactions from their unbelieving neighbors. The reason that most Christians are so ineffective and burned-out with so many problems is that they do not have knowledge about the Holy Spirit and what He can do in their lives.

The focus of this book is to explain to the layman the secret of how to be filled with the Spirit and how to daily walk in the Spirit, having a joyful, Spirit-filled life of service, lived to the glory of God. This book emphasizes important, biblical beliefs about the Spirit-filled life based only on the authority of the Word of God rather than on experience. These beliefs are centered only on the foundation of Jesus Christ's virgin birth, atonement for sin, and His bodily resurrection made available to individuals only by God's grace, working only through the Holy Spirit and received only by faith.

Most Christians realize that the Holy Spirit indwells them at the time they receive Christ, and most experience the joy of the Holy Spirit at that time, but few Christians benefit from the power, guidance, and fruit of the Holy Spirit in their daily lives. Most would like to be filled with the Holy Spirit and daily walk in the Spirit, but they do not know how to go about it. This book explains the three phases of the Holy Spirit in the Christian's life.

Receiving the Holy Spirit at salvation (Romans 8:9-14). For this event to happen, the person must repent of his sins, believe, and receive Jesus Christ as his Savior.

The filling of the Holy Spirit at dedication (Ephesians 5:18-19; Romans 12:1). The individual must abandon self and yield his life for service. He does this by identifying with Christ and surrendering control of his life to God.

Walking in the Holy Spirit in daily action (Galatians 5:16-25). For this to happen, the believer must confess his sin every day (I John 1:9), deny self (Luke 9:23), and obey the commandments of Christ (John 14:21; I John 3:23). He does this by abiding in Christ (John 15) and surrendering self. The Holy Spirit's filling then is renewed daily in a believer's life, and he has the power and guidance of the Holy Spirit for service, which results in spiritual fruit.

Daily living and walking in the Spirit are accomplished in the same way we started the Christian life. It is not by our own works, talents, or merit but by faith in Jesus Christ that He will work in and through us to do His will and build His body, the church. The Spirit-filled Christian decides to have the following:

- A willing walk—daily crucifying self and through his life by obedience letting the Holy Spirit reveal Christ's love and character, which provides holiness.

- A worthy walk—putting off sinful habits that damage relationships and putting on the disciplines of God's grace, which promotes unity in the body of Christ.
- A witnessing walk—using the gifts that the Holy Spirit has given at salvation and empowered at dedication to declare and reveal Christ's redemptive love to a lost and dying world, thus obeying Christ's great commission, which produces spiritual fruit.
- A faith walk—trusting in Christ and the promises in His Word, which promises victory.

In the 1940s and 1950s the Silver Publishing Company Foundation in Pittsburgh, Pennsylvania, reprinted and distributed over half a million free copies of the inspiring book *The Threefold Secret of the Holy Spirit* by James H. McConkey, written in 1887. It served as a model for chapters 2 through 4 of this book. The authors praise the Lord for the influence of the book on their understanding of the Spirit-filled life and walk more than fifty years ago.

It is the authors' desire that every Christian know how to live and walk the joyful Spirit-filled life of service and be a recipient of the power, joy, and spiritual fruit that only the Holy Spirit can give.

Chapter 1

# FUNDAMENTALS OF THE SPIRIT-FILLED LIFE

Average Christians know very little about the Holy Spirit and the way He works in the believer's life. As a consequence, they miss the comfort, control, edification, guidance, power for service, and victory of a Spirit-led walk with the Lord. They therefore live a stressful Christian life full of doubt, worry, fear, and confusion, with many of them ending up in a pastor's or counselor's office to find relief.

Some new believers, in their efforts to conquer sin, to counteract the influence of the flesh and the world, and to live a holy life, construct a list of extrabiblical rules. By exercising self-discipline, they attain a false but self-satisfying level of sanctification. They ignore the Holy Spirit's work in the sanctification process and depend on their ability to maintain a moral and upright life by keeping their self-imposed rules. These attempts often lead to failure, hypocrisy, or disappointment.

Some Christians substitute frantic gospel efforts and church activity in their misinterpretation of how to grow and serve the Lord in their church and soon suffer "burnout" and fall by the wayside. Pastors tend to foster this "Use them or lose them" approach, especially with new converts. They put the novices to work, getting them involved in junior church and nursery duty or signing them up to help in the parking lot or at the door as a welcome guide. Instead, these new Christians should be in

Sunday school and church, receiving teaching in the fundamental principles of the Bible.

Other very sincere Christians turn to health-and-wealth concepts of Christianity instead of considering sacrifice and service, which biblical Christianity requires. They also hope to experience the sign gifts, such as tongues and healing, which they expect to verify their possession of and blessing from the Holy Spirit.

A few believers, of a more mystical bent, daily spend hours in prayer, worship, and contemplation of the Word of God, seeking a more intimate walk with God and a holy life with victory over the world, the flesh, and the Devil. These things are important for Christians for growth and knowledge of the Word of God and are taught by Jesus in John 15:1-10, but they are no substitute for the filling and work of the Holy Spirit in the life of the believer. Only He will bring true spiritual satisfaction and victory.

All of the desires and longings of the searching Christians mentioned above can be realized only if they will learn the Bible truths about the Holy Spirit and let Him do the work in their lives that God sent Him to do. Such knowledge of the Holy Spirit should be grounded in the clear teaching of the eternal, verbally inspired Word of God alone and never on a person's emotional experience.

### Experience Replacing Biblical Authority

"Experience" is a recent trend gaining dominance in Christian circles, displacing scriptural authority, and even logical, medical, academic, and moral reason. Experience is the idea that an emotional experience in one's own life is a valid way of determining truth and God's purpose and plan. Many have used it even as a substitute for the truth of the Scriptures and depend almost entirely on it in their lives.

A problem with using subjective, feeling-oriented experience as a criterion for behavior and reality is that it makes us question all authority and principles of acceptable decorum. This questioning invites moral and mental confusion with possible demonic control.

Because personal experience is so frequently substituted for scriptural truth in the church and in society, it is important that we understand the difference between experience and biblical authority concerning the Holy Spirit's manifesting Himself in the believer's life.

Intense emotional experiences are affected by many factors and variables received from physical senses. A phrase, song, scene, caress, odor, taste, and even pain or pleasure can unleash memories and overwhelming emotions that can be mistaken for a spiritual experience. Brain tumors, high fevers, drugs, chemicals, and imbalanced hormones can result in abnormal brain function, which manifests itself in unusual and sometimes bizarre experiences. The Devil is adept at deceiving feeling-oriented Christians with unusual or supernatural experiences, visions, dreams, and realistic apparitions, such as the appearance of some human or an angel. Because personal experience is subject to such distortion, a person is in grave danger of serious error and deception when biblical authority is not used to discern and judge every matter.

When one person's experience happens to many people, it may become a doctrine or practice with no valid reference to the Scriptures. For example, one person starts hysterical laughing and the whole congregation begins laughing. This is attributed to the Holy Spirit and becomes a basic part of the church's form of worship. Or people begin to faint (being "slain in the Spirit") and this becomes an expected response and habitual practice. The fainting may be the result of hyperventilation. In many churches certain types of music (using a drum set and/or electric bass to give a syncopated beat) and specific styles of preaching (short, breathy, repeated phrases and prolonged vowel sounds) are used to "build a ramp," taking the emotions to an intense peak that demands release. The result is often weird imaginations, distorted thinking, wild delusions, and outlandish emotional behavior masquerading as spiritual experiences. Many churches encourage unrestrained emotional experiences such as barking, braying, shaking, wild dancing, and outlandish gyrations, which create pandemonium and closely resemble demonic activity.

Human emotion and its expressions vary widely depending on physiological makeup, culture, early childhood training, and environment. The Bible underscores this variety by recording people dancing, singing, shouting, weeping, clapping, and holding up the hands when publicly worshiping and praising God. However, I Corinthians 14, the chapter on tongues, gives general rules for worshiping God in all public services. We are to sing and pray with the Spirit and with understanding (v. 15). Worship is to edify others (v. 26). The spirits of the prophets are to be subject to the prophets (v. 32), worship should not lead to confusion (v. 33), and all things are to be done decently and in order (v. 40). Emotion and feelings do not precede or produce the manifestation of the Holy Spirit and the joy of the Lord but instead are the result of the Holy Spirit's indwelling, filling, and daily blessings.

Two hundred years ago Jonathan Edwards said, "Many godly persons have undoubtedly in this and other ages, exposed themselves to woeful delusions, by an aptness to lay too much weight on impulses and impressions, as if they were immediate revelations from God, to signify something future, or to direct them where to go, and what to do" (quoted in Hank Hanegraaff's *Counterfeit Revival*). Edwards described true conversions as "extraordinary works of God." Today, some religious leaders use that description to defend the bizarre manifestations in their services, which they encourage and heartily approve.

A variation of the emphasis on experiences is public confessions of sin, which many Christians consider to be the evidence of a genuine Holy Spirit revival, e.g., the college revivals in the 1940s and early 1950s and the revivals in the 1980s in Africa and the 1995-96 revivals in many evangelical colleges. The fleshly desire for attention and peer approval prompts many to reveal the lurid details of their sins. Others, in order to get mental relief from guilt, publicly confess all their sins and even their sinful, lustful desires and imaginations. These types of confessions draw a crowd of voyeuristic spectators and generate a snowball effect in the group. "Being transparent" is the modern term for public group confessional behavior that is being promoted in many churches and Bible study groups.

Public sin demands public confession, but it should be made in general terms without sordid details. Private sin requires only private confession to God. Scripture teaches that if we have wronged others we should immediately confess the sin to the wronged brother and be reconciled (Matthew 5:23, 24; 18:15-17; James 5:16). All confession of sin should be accompanied by genuine repentance, restitution, if necessary, and forgiveness with restoration by the wronged individual or group.

Awakenings or revivals in America's history that produced long-lasting changes in individuals, churches, and whole communities were centered on prayer and strong Bible preaching against sin rather than on feeling-oriented experience and public confessions. Many modern preachers defend their lack of preaching on sin by saying that they are called to preach a positive gospel of love and not a gospel of legalism that makes people feel guilty.

The ministry of Jonathan Edwards was characterized by dynamic expositional preaching. The message of the modern revival is characterized by experiential revelations and prophecies unrelated to the clear teaching of the Scriptures. Crediting our unscriptural experiences, teaching, and practices to the Lord is nothing less than the denial of His truth and a slander of God Himself. New Christians can avoid much confusion about receiving and being filled with the Holy Spirit if they concentrate on the teaching of the apostles (repentance and faith in Christ, Acts 2:38) rather than on the experience of the apostles at Pentecost (the mighty wind, cloven tongues of fire, and speaking in tongues of a foreign language, Acts 2:2-4). Trying to duplicate anyone's experience ends only in frustration and disappointment.

### Bible Principles About the Holy Spirit

There are certain foundational Bible principles about the Holy Spirit. We must base our thinking on them and use them to evaluate a Spirit-filled life and any spiritual experiences or seemingly miraculous phenomena. These principles have been compiled from Charles Ryrie's *Basic Theology* and other conservative Bible doctrine textbooks and are as follows:

1. **The Holy Spirit is a person.** He is the third person of the Trinity, and, as Jesus promised in John 14:16-17, He was sent as the comforter, or paraclete (someone called alongside the believer). He is not just a divine energy and power, but He is also a person with intelligence (I Corinthians 2:10-11) and a mind (Romans 8:27). He is a person with feelings, who can be grieved and insulted (Ephesians 4:30; Hebrews 10:29). He is also a person with a will, who directs the activities of believers (Acts 15:6-11) and distributes gifts to the body of Christ (I Corinthians 12:11). He can perform miracles (Acts 8:39). He intercedes for the believer (Romans 8:26).

2. **The Holy Spirit is God.** He has all the essence of God, He proceeds from the Father and the Son, and He is associated on an equal basis with the Father and the Son (Matthew 8:19; II Corinthians 13:14). Sixteen times He is related by name to the other two persons of the Trinity (John 15:26). He possesses the same attributes of God: omniscience (I Corinthians 2:11), omnipresence (Psalm 139:7), and omnipotence (Psalm 33:4).

   He was the agent giving the inspired Word of God (I Peter 1:21). He was involved in the creation of the world (Genesis 1:2). He was the cause of the virgin birth (Luke 1:35).

3. **The Holy Spirit always glorifies Christ and never Himself (John 16:14).** One of Christ's last promises given in John 16:13-14 was that He would send a teacher to guide the believer into all truth and that He would glorify Jesus Christ. Jesus Christ, and not the Holy Spirit, is to have the preeminence (Colossians 1:18-19). Jesus Christ, the Son, was appointed heir to all things and upholds all things by the word of His power (Hebrews 1:2-3).

4. **It is the ministry of the Holy Spirit to live out the life of Christ in the believer as he progressively attains sanctification (conformity to the image of Christ) to be finally realized in heaven (I Corinthians 4:11; Philippians 1:20-21; Romans 8:29).** The Holy Spirit performs this ministry by doing the following:

  • Convicting: The Holy Spirit convicts the sinner of his sin, God's righteousness, and the coming judgment by using his unbelief and the law, the Ten Commandments, to bring him to repentance and salvation (John 16:7-8; Galatians 4:24-26). The Holy Spirit convicts the Christian of sin by using Christ's two new commandments of faith and love to bring him to repentance, confession, and restored fellowship (I John 3:23; Matthew 22:37-39; I John 1:7-10).

  • Assuring: The Holy Spirit gives assurance to the believer by sealing him until the day of redemption (Ephesians 4:30), presenting the earnest of the Spirit as a guarantee of redemption (Ephesians 1:13-14), and serves as the element in which Christ baptizes him into the spiritual body of Christ, signifying His indwelling (John 1:33; I Corinthians 12:13).

  • Teaching: The Holy Spirit's teaching ministry, which began at Pentecost, will continue until the Rapture (John 16:12-15; I Corinthians 2:13). His teaching contains all the truth about Christ. He also teaches in Scripture about things to come by prophecy. His anointing of the believer and giving the gifts of teaching to the teachers and preachers clearly reveal a believer's understanding of the work of God (I John 2:27; Romans 12:7). He teaches Christians to renew their mind and restrain the flesh as they progress toward the goal of being conformed to the image of Jesus Christ (Romans 12:2; 8:13).

• Guiding: The believer is free to ask directions for his life and is confident that the Holy Spirit will give guidance (Proverbs 3:5-6). He is led by His inner presence rather than by outward pressures (Romans 8:14). He guides the Spirit-filled believer in maintaining right relationships with other believers to bring about unity in the body of Christ (Ephesians 4:1-16).

• Praying: The Holy Spirit prays and intercedes for the believer (Romans 8:26-27). Because of weakness, believers' prayers are imperfect. They do not always know what to pray for and how to pray. The Holy Spirit always prays according to the Word of God.

5. **There are three phases of the Holy Spirit and His relation to the life of the believer.**

*Table 1*
**The Holy Spirit**

|  | *Salvation Receiving the Holy Spirit* | *Dedication Filling of the Holy Spirit* | *Daily Action Walking in the Holy Spirit* |
|---|---|---|---|
| *The individual acts as a result of the Holy Spirit's conviction.* | Repents and believes Receives Christ Surrenders sins | Abandons self and yields Identifies with Christ Surrenders life | Confesses, denies self, and obeys Abides in Christ Surrenders self |

| *The Holy Spirit reacts as a result of God's grace.* | Enters<br>Gives joy | Takes full possession<br>Produces fruit | Is renewed<br>Gives power and guidance for service |
| --- | --- | --- | --- |
| | | | |

## Phase 1

Receiving the Holy Spirit at the time of salvation, when the Holy Spirit comes into the personal life and body of the believer (Romans 8:9-14; I Corinthians 6:19-20). For this to happen, the individual must first of all repent of his sins, believe, and receive Jesus Christ as personal Savior. At that same time he also surrenders his sin. The Holy Spirit then enters the person's life, and the believer experiences the joy of the Holy Spirit.

## Phase 2

Filling of the Holy Spirit at dedication, when the Holy Spirit assumes full control of the believer's life (Romans 12:1-2; Ephesians 5:18-19; 2:4-7). The individual must abandon self and yield his life for service. He does this by identifying with Christ and surrendering control of his life to God (Galatians 2:20; Romans 12:1-2). The Holy Spirit then takes full possession and gives the believer the fruit of the Holy Spirit (Galatians 5:22-23), which is the manifestation of the Holy Spirit filling one's life. The Holy Spirit also empowers the gift(s) of the Spirit that we received at salvation (I Corinthians 12:4-11).

## Phase 3

Walking in the Holy Spirit in daily life, when the Holy Spirit guides the believer and gives power for service (Galatians 5:16-25). For this to happen, the individual believer must confess his sin every day (I John 1:9), deny self (Luke 9:23), and obey the commandments of Christ (John 14:21). He does this by daily abiding in Christ (John 15:1-16). The Holy Spirit then is renewed daily in a believer's life, and the believer has the power and guidance of the Holy Spirit for service.

Most Christians are ineffective and burdened with many problems because they do not know and understand about the Holy Spirit and what He can do in their lives. Chapter 2 explains phase 1, the indwelling, or baptism, of the Holy Spirit. Chapter 3 details phase 2, the filling of the Holy Spirit, and chapter 4 gives instruction on phase 3, how to walk willingly in the Spirit. Chapter 5 explains how to have a worthy walk that promotes unity in the church. Chapter 6 discusses the Spirit-filled life and the witness of the gospel. Chapter 7 clarifies the faith walk that assures victory, chapter 8 deals with the active gifts of the Spirit for the believer, and chapter 9 discusses the inactive sign gifts.

The appropriation of the filling of the Holy Spirit in one's life is the greatest tool a mature believer has for effectively converting sinners and helping the saints to be edified and solve life's problems. Most Christians realize that the Holy Spirit indwells them at the time they receive Christ, and most experience the joy of the Holy Spirit at the time of salvation, but few Christians realize the benefits of turning their lives over to the control of the Holy Spirit. Pray that the Holy Spirit will give you wisdom to know and understand how to be filled with the Spirit and how to have the power, guidance, and fruit of the blessed Holy Spirit in your daily life. It is the only way to be effective in the Lord's service and to have a ministry that glorifies the Lord (I Corinthians 10:31).

Chapter 2

# THE INDWELLING OF THE HOLY SPIRIT AT SALVATION

## PHASE 1

The first phase of a person's union with the Holy Spirit begins at salvation when the Holy Spirit indwells the believer. The Holy Spirit comes into a life the minute a person receives Christ, to conform that one to the image of Christ and enable him to exhibit God's love, grace, and attributes through his actions and deeds (Romans 8:29; Ephesians 2:10).

### *Salvation: Conviction, and Revelation of God's Love*

One's first contact with the Holy Spirit occurs before salvation and is twofold. (1) The Holy Spirit reveals God's righteousness and judgment and convicts all humans of their sin (John 16:8). (2) The Holy Spirit is also responsible for making plain the truths of God's love and plan of salvation to all who desire to know God.

**Principle 1: Jesus promises that the Holy Spirit prepares a man's heart for salvation through conviction of sin and unbelief and through a clear awareness of the urgent need of a Savior.** "And when he [the Holy Spirit] is come, he will reprove [convict] the world of sin, and of righteousness, and of judgment" (John 16:8-11). This teaching of Jesus to His disciples recognizes the major problem that unsaved people have in coming to the Lord. In themselves they lack a deep conviction of their lost, sinful condition and of the eternal punishment that awaits those whose sins are not cleansed and forgiven by God. Thus, they have no conviction in their hearts of a need to be saved from anything. It is unfortunately true that some preachers have not helped with this problem. They have fallen into the error of suggesting that it is not necessary to emphasize man's sin and God's judgment when giving the gospel. They believe in preaching only a "gospel of love," which doesn't demean a person's self-concept. Thus, they offer a confusing gospel and a false hope to unsaved people.

All of the people of the world are hopelessly lost in sin and bound for an eternity of punishment and separation from God if they die without the Lord Jesus Christ in their lives. This sinful, lost condition includes the openly wicked person, who lives in total rebellion against God (Romans 1:18-32); the self-righteous person, who believes that everyone else may be lost but that he himself is too righteous to have any need for God's forgiveness and salvation (Romans 2:1-16); and the Jew, who believes that he is one of God's own people with so much knowledge of God and favor from His hand that he is already qualified to go to heaven (Romans 2:17–3:8; Philippians 3:4-6).

God describes those in this sinful, lost condition in a number of passages. Romans 3:9 concludes that "they are all under sin." Romans 3:23 states that "all have sinned, and come short of the glory of God." Romans 6:23 says that "the wages of sin is death." Ephesians 2:3 closes with the phrase "and were by nature the children of wrath, even as others."

In spite of all the teaching from the Scriptures concerning our lost condition, we, in ourselves, would still have no personal conviction of sin and would feel no need to come to the Savior. Were it not for the convicting work of the Holy Spirit, who penetrates and prepares our hearts, none of us would be willing to face the fact of our sin, much less repent of it and trust the Lord as our only Savior from sin.

## *Salvation: The New Birth (John 3:1-21)*

**Principle 2: God builds upon a clear knowledge of the truth to bring men and women into a saving relationship with Him.** "Ye shall know the truth, and the truth shall make you free" (John 8:32); "so then, faith cometh by hearing, and hearing by the word of God" (Romans 10:17). In His interview with Nicodemus, Jesus is dealing with a man who has a thorough knowledge of Old Testament Scriptures. Jesus then proceeds to build upon that foundation with additional truth so that it is finally clear to Nicodemus not only that he needs the new spiritual birth but also that Jesus alone can give that new birth to him (John 3:1-21).

In dealing with Nicodemus, Jesus emphasizes that no matter how devotedly and strictly people live their lives, no one can please God or qualify for God's salvation on the basis of the old nature. As Nicodemus, in ignorance, continues to insist on approaching God on the basis of the birth and the nature he already has, Jesus, in reply, five times repeats the necessity for Nicodemus and everyone else in the world to be given a new spiritual nature by God and to be accepted by God on the basis of that new nature.

Thus, to be born and live our lives in the flesh (the water birth), no matter what human efforts we might make to please God, is never to reach God because we are in the sinful human realm. God will accept us only on the basis of the second birth (the spiritual birth), which is in the spiritual realm and which can come only as we are "born again" by the Spirit of God. This birth alone qualifies us to have a relationship with God and to live with Him eternally.

## *Salvation: Believing and Receiving Jesus Christ*

**Principle 3: The spiritual birth and eternal life with God in heaven come only through repentance for our sins and sincere belief in Jesus Christ as our Savior and Lord (John 3:14-36).** "That whosoever believeth in him should not perish, but have eternal life. For God so loved the world, that he gave his only begotten Son, that whosoever believeth in him should not perish, but have everlasting life. For God sent not his Son into the world to condemn the world; but that the world through him might be saved. He that believeth on him is not condemned: but he that believeth not is condemned already, because he hath not believed in the name of the only begotten Son of God. . . . He that believeth on the Son hath everlasting life: and he that believeth not the Son shall not see life; but the wrath of God abideth on him" (John 3:15-18, 36).

These verses state that the only escape from eternal punishment (in hell) is to believe on the Lord Jesus Christ and receive everlasting life (heaven).

### *Salvation: Believing Certain Truths*

**Principle 4: To believe on the Lord Jesus Christ implies acceptance of certain Bible truths about man and Jesus Christ.** "For I delivered unto you first of all that which I also received, how that Christ died for our sins according to the scriptures; and that he was buried, and that he rose again the third day according to the scriptures" (I Corinthians 15:3-4). And they said, Believe on the Lord Jesus Christ, and thou shalt be saved, and thy house" (Acts 16:31).

1. Man is a sinner and must face the judgment for his sins (Romans 3:23; 6:23).
2. Man cannot save himself by his own works or by "turning over a new leaf" or by joining some church (John 1:13; Ephesians 2:8-9).
3. Jesus Christ is God (John 10:30) and is the virgin-born Son of God (Luke 1:30-35).
4. Jesus Christ (God's Son) died on the cross for man's sin, shedding His precious blood as the payment for sin (Ephesians 1:7).

5. Jesus Christ is the resurrected Savior, who has power to save from sin because of His resurrection (I Corinthians 15:20-23; II Corinthians 4:14).

To make eternal salvation a part of your life, you must make the following decision: I must repent (turn from my sins) and believe (have faith) in Jesus Christ as my Savior by receiving Him into my life (Luke 13:3; John 1:12-13). Jesus Christ then comes into my life (Colossians 1:27) and becomes my righteousness (I Corinthians 1:30) and my assurance of eternal life in heaven (I John 5:11-13). The moment I receive Christ I am born again spiritually (John 1:12-13), my eternal life begins (John 3:15, 36), and the Holy Spirit indwells me, making my body His temple (I Corinthians 6:19-20).

### Salvation: Baptized by the Holy Spirit into the Body of Christ

**Principle 5: Jesus Christ guarantees our salvation by baptizing us through the Spirit into the body of Christ.** "For ye are all children of God by faith in Christ Jesus. For as many of you as have been baptized into Christ have put on Christ. There is neither Jew nor Greek, there is neither bond nor free, there is neither male nor female: for ye are all one in Christ Jesus" (Galatians 3:26-28; I Corinthians 12:12-13; John 1:33).

These passages are clearly teaching that the baptism of the Holy Spirit is related to our being brought into the body of Christ. Christ's spiritual body is composed of believers all over the world, who are united by the baptism of the Holy Spirit into one body of believers. This includes all born-again Christians of all types of backgrounds and periods of time. This happens at the moment of salvation and does not involve some extra experience or the ordinance of water baptism. It is accomplished by the Holy Spirit and is final. Local church-member relationships may change, but our relationship with the spiritual body of Christ is unchangeable and irrevocable.

Many believe that the term "baptism of the Holy Spirit" refers to some special anointing of the Holy Spirit at a later point in a person's life after that person has already been saved. Many link this with speaking in tongues and other special manifestations of the Spirit. The idea seems to be that we are saved when we first trust Christ as our only Savior from sin but that our lives are still incomplete until we have experienced the baptism of the Holy Spirit. These views are unscriptural because the Scriptures give an entirely different meaning to the term.

### *Salvation: Our Assurance*

**Principle 6: The basis for the assurance of our eternal salvation and of going to heaven when we die is the sealing work of the Holy Spirit and the promises of God.** "My sheep hear my voice, and I know them, and they follow me: and I give unto them eternal life; and they shall never perish, neither shall any man pluck them out of my hand. My Father, which gave them me, is greater than all; and no man is able to pluck them out of my Father's hand. I and my Father are one" (John 10:27-30).

In this section of Scripture, Jesus is teaching that, in salvation, we not only belong to Him but we also can never have this relationship with Him taken away. It is an eternal relationship. We will always be His sheep. Below are twenty Bible promises that tell us what God does when we receive Christ into our life.

### *Twenty Bible Promises of Assurance*
- I am a child of God (John 1:12-13).
- I have started living forever (John 3:16).
- I am held in God's and Christ's hand (John 10:28-29).
- I have a place prepared for me (John 14:1-3).
- I am justified forever (Romans 5:1).
- I am forever joined to Christ (Romans 6:5).
- I have no condemnation (Romans 8:1).

- I am vitally linked to the Father (Romans 8:15-16).
- I have my righteousness and my redemption in Christ (I Corinthians 1:30).
- I am set apart to God (I Corinthians 6:11).
- I am united to all believers (I Corinthians 12:12-13).
- I am declared righteous (II Corinthians 5:21).
- I am identified with Christ (Ephesians 2:5-7).
- I am His workmanship (Ephesians 2:10).
- I have God's power within me (Ephesians 3:20).
- I am sealed by the Holy Spirit (Ephesians 4:30).
- I am a citizen of heaven (Philippians 3:20).
- I am complete in Christ (Colossians 2:9-10).
- I am in God's kingdom (I Thessalonians 2:12).
- I have an inheritance reserved for me (I Peter 1:4).

The promises of God, however, are closely linked to the work that the Holy Spirit did for us at that moment we put our faith in Jesus Christ as our Savior and were indwelt by the Holy Spirit. At that moment, He sealed us forever in our salvation and in our relationship with God. Thus, we have assurance not only because God has promised that our relationship with Him is an eternal one but also because He has acted in our lives, by the work of the Holy Spirit, to finalize and make that relationship secure.

This sealing work of the Holy Spirit is taught in many passages, and all of them are given for the purpose of assuring us that, when we have put our faith in the Lord as our only Savior from sin, we need not doubt or fear for our salvation.

"Now he which stablisheth us with you in Christ, and hath anointed us, is God; who hath also sealed us and given us the earnest [pledge] of the Spirit in our hearts" (II Corinthians 1:21-22).

"In whom ye also trusted, after that ye heard the word of truth, the gospel of your salvation: in whom also after that ye believed, ye were sealed with that holy Spirit of promise, which is the earnest of our inheritance until the redemption of the purchased possession, unto the praise of his glory. . . . And grieve not the holy Spirit of God, whereby ye are sealed unto the day of redemption" (Ephesians 1:13-14; 4:30).

Real assurance comes as the new believer thanks God for what has already been accomplished in his life at salvation rather than praying for God to do what he imagines God ought to do. One's assurance of eternal life in heaven is based on the promises of God given in His Word (I John 5:11-13) and not on how one feels.

### *Salvation: Test*

Everyone must ask himself the following questions:

1. Have I acknowledged my sin and repented?
2. Do I believe that Jesus Christ, God's Son, shed His blood on the cross as a payment for my sins, was resurrected, and will give me eternal life in heaven if I believe on Him?
3. Have I received Jesus Christ into my life, and am I depending on Him alone for my eternal life?

If you can answer *yes* to these questions on the authority of the Word of God, you are a born-again Christian and the Holy Spirit indwells you to comfort and guide throughout your life. The following six ideas will help you live and grow in the Christian faith:

1. Make a public declaration of your faith by being baptized.
2. Join and attend a local Bible believing and preaching church.
3. Give a tithe (ten percent) of your income to the local church.
4. Establish a daily time of Bible reading, prayer, and worship.
5. Begin reaching out to others by sharing your faith with them and backing it up with good deeds.
6. Live a Spirit-filled life of service to the Lord.

## *Summary*

These are summary truths that serve as the foundation of the Spirit-filled life when you accept Christ as your Savior. (1) The Holy Spirit indwells you. (2) He is the life of Christ in you. (3) He is willing and able to produce the character of Christ through you. (4) Jesus Christ and His Word become the object and focus of your faith.

The following chapter gives the Bible way of being filled with the Holy Spirit.

# Chapter 3

# FILLING OF THE HOLY SPIRIT

## PHASE 2

B orn-again Christians down through church history, but especially in the last two centuries, have been desirous of experiencing the peaceful, powerful, and eternally effective abundant life in Christ that Jesus promised in John 10:10. They have been frustrated in their quest by the increasing secularization of Christian society; the superficial theology preached from many pulpits, which focuses on meeting the needs of self-centered Christians; and the inroads into the church of humanistic philosophy, which enthrones man instead of God as the center of the universe.

### *Spirit Filling: The Abundant Life*

Jesus says in John 10:10, "I am come that they might have life, and that they might have it more abundantly." Abundant life is not found on the physical plane expressed, as the world views it, in money, power, possessions, position, prestige, and success. Instead, Jesus is referring to the spiritual plane from His kingdom of God viewpoint, which is righteousness, peace, and joy in the Holy Ghost (Romans 10:17). In John 10, Jesus declares Himself the way of salvation in verse 9 and follows in verses 10 and 11 with a description of Himself as the Shepherd and His sheep as the born-again Christians experiencing the abundant life.

Following the Shepherd in complete submission and trust brings protection, provision, and the peace of Psalm 23 and John 14:27. It also brings the *love* of John 15:9-10, the *joy* of John 15:11, the *power* of Philippians 4:13, the *above all that we ask or think* of Ephesians 3:20, and the *all things work together for good* of Romans 8:28. This is the abundant life—to know and be identified with Christ in all of His fullness. The abundant life might be compared to the ocean. Storms may rage and cold winds may howl, temporarily disturbing the surface. But in the depths everything is calm, serene, and undisturbed with a constant temperature prevailing and the gentle currents moving in one direction. The Spirit-filled Christian immerses himself in the ocean of God's love and moves through this life in the peaceful current of God's grace that carries him to heaven. The abundant life is experienced and lived by being filled with the Holy Spirit.

*The Filling of the Holy Spirit Defined*

Spirit filling is both God's sovereign empowering and guiding by the Spirit for special ministry and the Spirit's filling with the character of Jesus Christ. The fruit of the Spirit that will be produced in a Spirit-filled life is a description of the attributes of Christlikeness (Galatians 5:22-23).

The biblical command in Ephesians 5:18, "be filled with the spirit," does not refer to a life filled with a quantity, for the Holy Spirit is a person and does not come into a life by graduated amounts. He comes into a life at salvation and never leaves. In the context of Ephesians 5:18, "filled with the spirit" means controlled by the Spirit. As a drunkard's behavior is controlled by an excess of wine, so the Christian is commanded to be controlled by the Holy Spirit.

How much of his life is the believer going to let the Holy Spirit control? It is not a question of one's having all of the Holy Spirit but rather the Holy Spirit's having all of him? Who is on the throne of his life? It is the one who has the control: either self or the Holy Spirit.

*Biblical Descriptions*

Many terms have been used to label the means to achieve abundant life: a Spirit-filled life (Ephesians 5:18), the crucified life (Galatians 2:20), an exchanged life (first used by Hudson Taylor, John 15:1-5), the fruitful life (Galatians 5:22-23), identification with Christ (Ephesians 2:4-7), the transformed life (Romans 12:1-2), the deeper life (Luke 5:4), and a victorious life (I John 5:4-5). The authors prefer to use the more descriptive phrase "the Spirit-filled life" along with the terms "crucified life" and "identification with Christ" as the means to accomplish the goal of the abundant life in Christ. There is general agreement among theologians that abandonment of self and complete dedication of one's life is necessary for a person to be filled with (controlled by) the Spirit, an essential to living the abundant life.

*Personal Descriptions*

V. Raymond Edman, in his book *They Found the Secret,* reviewed biographies of twenty leading Christians in the last five hundred years, including John Bunyan, Amy Carmichael, Dwight L. Moody, Andrew Murray, Hudson Taylor, Charles G. Trumbill, and Walter L. Wilson. Although of various theological persuasions, they had one thing in common. They had all reached a point in their lives when the indwelling of the Lord Jesus Christ was made real and rewarding by the filling of the Holy Spirit. From then on they experienced the abundant life by surrendering self and their own efforts and drawing on the unfailing resources of the Lord Jesus Christ. Edman found that the events to achieve this Spirit-controlled life, although varied in detail, were very similar:

1. A pattern of defeat, disappointment, and powerlessness followed by a deep desire for God's close presence and power.

2.A dedication of one's life for the Lord's service and eternal things accompanied by an utter surrender of self.

3.An asking for and appropriation by faith of Christ's resurrected life with His power and His mighty presence.

4.A renewed sense of the Holy Spirit's presence, power, and guidance as He operates through one's life in an expanded, fruitful ministry.

These points drawn from the experiences of these godly Spirit-filled saints are reflected in the detailed discussion of the Four Biblical Steps below, describing how to be filled with the Holy Spirit.

### *How to Be Filled with the Holy Spirit*

*Step 1. Desire*

Jesus said, "Blessed are they which do hunger and thirst after righteousness: for they shall be filled" (Matthew 5:6). The psalmist expressed the desire in Psalm 63:1-2, "my soul thirsteth for thee, my flesh longeth for thee in a dry and thirsty land, where no water is; to see thy power and thy glory." In the church age a wholehearted desire for the fullness of Christ is necessary for a person to be filled with the Holy Spirit. Do you really desire God's righteousness, holiness, love, and power to take over and replace the self life? Are you willing to crucify the flesh with all the desires of the self life and have Christ's love and righteousness fill your life (Galatians 5:24)?

*Step 2. Dedication*

"I beseech you therefore, brethren, by the mercies of God, that ye present your bodies a living sacrifice, holy, acceptable unto God, which is your reasonable service. And be not conformed to this world: but be ye transformed by the renewing of your mind, that ye may prove what is that good, and acceptable, and perfect, will of God" (Romans 12:1-2). "I am crucified with Christ: nevertheless I live; yet not I, but Christ liveth in me: and the life which I now live in the flesh I live by the faith of the Son of God, who loved me, and gave himself for me" (Galatians 2:20).

All Christians are urged by God to present their bodies for full-time service to God and to let the Holy Spirit transform them by the renewing of their mind (Romans 12:1-2). Dedication requires an initial decision of the presentation of your life to God, giving Him full control. A few people make this decision when they accept Christ as their Savior. Most Christians, however, do it sometime after their salvation, usually within two or three years. The dedicated believer decides to daily crucify self and submit himself in obedience to God's control, His Word, and His will, thus being empowered or strengthened by the Holy Spirit to accomplish righteous works and the will of God (Galatians 2:20; Luke 9:23).

Do you want to have the Lord set all plans for your life? Do you want the Holy Spirit to control every action and reaction? Do you want to be possessed by Him? Do you want your character and personality to be taken over and gradually changed to be like Christ? Are you willing without any reservations to go anywhere and do anything God wants you to do? If your answer is yes to these questions, you simply present your body in its entirety, including your mind, to God's complete control. That is what He asks you to do.

Are you willing to make this life-changing decision? Then pray and make a dedication vow to God, make it known to others, and daily live this vow as you walk in the Spirit.

### Step 3. Ask

"And I say unto you, Ask, and it shall be given you; seek, and ye shall find; knock, and it shall be opened unto you. For every one that asketh receiveth; and he that seeketh findeth; and to him that knocketh it shall be opened. If a son shall ask bread of any of you that is a father, will he give him a stone? or if he ask a fish, will he for a fish give him a serpent? Or if he shall ask an egg, will he offer him a scorpion?" (Luke 11:9-11). Christ tells us to ask for the filling of the Spirit. We are not to ask Him to indwell us or come upon us. If we have trusted Christ as our Savior, the Holy Spirit already indwells us (Romans 8:16). Rather, we are to ask the Holy Spirit to fill our lives with His power and take full control. We do this without any doubts, excuses, or periods of pleading; simply ask and you will receive. Then thank Him for filling you (I Thessalonians 5:18).

*Step 4. Have faith*

"As ye have therefore received Christ Jesus the Lord, so walk ye in him" (Colossians 2:6). We receive Christ (the Holy Spirit comes into the life at that time) by faith. We also receive the filling of the Holy Spirit by faith. A person should not look for any feeling or physical manifestation or unusual signs. However, most report increased and lasting feelings of love, joy, peace, and humility of varied degrees, depending on one's emotional makeup that affect his actions and lifestyle (Galatians 5:22-24).

In summary, the doorway to the filling of the Holy Spirit and the resulting abundant life that bears much fruit is twofold.

- Turn your life over completely to God, submitting to His full control as a slave does to his master, and let Him be the Lord of your life (Romans 12:1-2; Ephesians 6:5-6).
- Daily crucify the flesh, where self rules and reigns (Galatians 5:24; Luke 9:23).

The decision is yours.

### The Self Life

Most Christians realize that they are not immune from exhibiting self-serving, unloving, sinful behavior. They sometimes resort to sarcasm, cutting remarks, humiliating others, proud boasting, vulgarity, unreasonableness, prejudice, and angry outbursts. The cure for this self-centered, fleshly conduct is being filled with the Holy Spirit, resulting in humble, loving servanthood. Christians understand that even though the Holy Spirit dwells within them they still have a sin tendency that will remain in them until they die. The Devil, with whom we are in constant warfare after salvation, uses this tendency to entice the Christian to be self-exalting and self-assertive, going his own way instead of God's way. He also uses carnal desires and the pressures of the world to tempt a Christian to go against God's will. The results are self-gratification or loving and serving self instead of God and others. This tendency is often referred to as *self* or, as the Bible states in Romans 7:17-25, *the flesh* or *the law of sin*. It is the technique believers use to meet their own needs by depending on their abilities and resources instead of Christ. To walk after the flesh is to live a lifestyle that does not depend on Christ and does not glorify God. It is refusing to allow Christ to work in and through him to do God's will and His pleasure (Philippians 2:13).

As new creatures in Christ we are separated from sin's dominion that serves unrighteousness. By Christ's death and by His resurrection, we are free from sin's domination to live and to serve righteousness (Romans 6:2-10). If we walk in the Spirit, our new nature in Christ has the power of the Holy Spirit for daily victory over sin and the flesh (Galatians 5:16). The flesh brings certain pleasure, satisfactions, and fulfillment of our selfish desires, which build up and enhance the self life. Preschool children are good examples of the self life. They are normally selfish and self-centered. Their favorite words are "me" and "mine," expressed in a variety of ways. Life centers around them and they are "takers" instead of "givers." Teens and adults have more refined ways of expressing the self life. Some typical examples are as follows:

- We, as Christians, feel pleasure when we think that our immediate selfish desires are satisfied. When not satisfied, we either pout or whine.

41

- We experience the quickening pulse and glow of an illicit affair, whether real or imagined or vicariously viewed on television.
- We scheme and use all manner of deceit to get our own way. When thwarted, we lash out in anger with verbal or physical abuse.
- We react to damaged relationships with self pity and bitterness.
- We respond to the thrill of competition with hostility and take great pride in soundly defeating the opposition, whether an individual or a team.
- We covet and get excited about acquiring more money, possessions, or power.
- We cleave to our corrupt habits and addictions, which we excuse but surely enjoy, even though they harm the body and soul.

*Evidences of the Self Life*

There are many evidences of the self life and they can be conveniently categorized into four groups.

**Manipulation and Use of People.** Early in life, children learn some of the following techniques to manipulate parents and teachers into giving them their own way.

- Questioning, arguing, and finally ignoring the rule, procedure, or assignment.
- Playing the strict parent or teacher against the lenient parent or teacher.
- Passively resisting by procrastinating or doing chores or school assignments hurriedly and sloppily.
- Emotionally and physically distancing by pouting, sulking, and isolating with bitterness.

Teens, as they move into adulthood, learn more sophisticated ways of manipulating people, such as flattery, tears, anger, and camouflaged bribes. Most adults who manipulate people also use one or more of the above techniques.

**Selfishness.** A "me first" attitude predominates. Self does not want to sacrifice time, talents, possessions, or money for the sake of others. It wants the glory and attention and is jealous when others receive awards and recognition.

**Self-indulgence.** The comfort zone is very important and bodily desires are dominant. The self is easily given to addictions, be it food, drugs, pornography, or television viewing. Lust is evident and leads to fornication and other sensual sins.

**Pride.** Self is never satisfied or content but always wants more. It wants power, position, and prestige with money as a motivating factor. Relationships and communications are filled with anger, bitterness, backbiting, complaining, ridicule, sarcasm, and lack of forgiveness. It has a critical spirit against others and is vindictive. Self rebels against control by authority and demands its rights.

*Victory over the Self Life*

For the sinner, the progression and end of the self life is described in Romans 1:18-32. All Christians after salvation have to struggle between serving Christ and serving self, much as Paul described his struggle in Romans 7:15-25. The only way to have victory with this struggle is to be filled with the Holy Spirit by making a total commitment, as a bond slave of Christ, to serve Christ and others. The biblical remedy for a lifestyle that enthrones self is walking in the Spirit resulting in loving, **humble servanthood**. It is also the key to strengthening relationships in the church, in marriage, in friendships, and even in contacts with the unsaved. Walking in the Spirit will be discussed in the next four chapters.

Chapter 4

# THE WILLING SPIRIT-FILLED WALK THAT PROVIDES HOLINESS

PHASE 3

After salvation with the concurrent indwelling of the Holy Spirit and dedication with the accompanying filling of the Spirit follows the third phase—walking in the Spirit, or willingly living the Spirit-filled life. "That the righteousness of the law might be fulfilled in us, who walk not after the flesh, but after the Spirit. For they that are after the flesh do mind the things of the flesh; but they that are after the Spirit the things of the Spirit" (Romans 8:4-5). "If we live in the Spirit, let us also walk in the Spirit. . . . Walk in the Spirit, and ye shall not fulfil the lust of the flesh" (Galatians 5:25, 16). Two key principles to daily walking in the Spirit are (1) loving God with all your heart, mind, and soul by identifying with Christ, having communion with Him, and being willingly obedient to His Word (2) and loving others as yourself and willingly submitting to the needs of others by maintaining a submissive, humble servant attitude (Ephesians 5:21).

*Loving God by Identification and Communion with Christ*
    **Principle 1: Loving God with all your heart, mind, and soul is accomplished by identifying Christ as the Lord of your life and**

**letting Him work His will in you and through you (Philippians 2:13).**
The identification with Christ principle is simply Christ in
you and you in Christ, a transaction that occurred at the time
of salvation. After becoming aware of this fact, you decide to
present your body to Christ in complete submission to His
control, letting Christ live His life in and through you (John
14:20; II Corinthians 5:17; Colossians 1:27; 3:12-17). The
identification with Jesus Christ is acknowledged by Paul in
Galatians 2:20. Paul identified with the death, burial, and
resurrection of Jesus Christ. Our body and its members should
have the same identification with Christ (Romans 6:10-13).
Further identification is given in Ephesians 2:4-7. This
identification is not by our own works but due to God's grace
and appropriated by faith at salvation (Ephesians 2:8-10). An
enlargement of the identification principle is given by Paul in
his prayer for the believers to have a full knowledge of Christ's
love (Ephesians 3:17-21). To know and to be identified with
Christ in all of His fullness and power of His resurrection, we
must also be willing to know the fellowship of His suffering
(Philippians 3:8-10). Scripture says that if we believe on Him
we shall also suffer with Him (Philippians 1:29). When we
arm ourselves with the same mind as the crucified Christ,
who shed His blood for us, and cease from following the
world's sin pattern, we will have the power and grace to
victoriously endure any suffering, persecution, and rejection
(I Peter 4:1-4). Most Christians, however, are unaware of this
"identification with Christ" truth until they dedicate their
bodies and submit to God's complete control of their lives.
The Holy Spirit then gives them the power to make this truth
a daily reality in their lives.

After realizing the identification principle and their intimate
union with Christ, Christians are eager for communion with
Christ through His Word, prayer, thanksgiving, praise, and

meditation (John 15:1-7). They desire His holiness, fullness, and presence, which give them the power through the Holy Spirit to conquer the self life, which is energized by the lusts of the flesh and pride, and to obey His Word (John 14:21). This desire is expressed by psalms, hymns, spiritual songs, and melodies flowing from the joyful Spirit-filled heart (Colossians 3:16). It is also expressed by thanksgiving in every situation (Ephesians 5:19-20; I Thessalonians 5:18). The Holy Spirit uses communion with Christ to give us the power to put on the attributes of Christ mentioned in Colossians 3:12-17 and to bring us to Christlikeness, which is our ultimate goal. We reflect Christ as we exhibit the fruit of the Spirit (Galatians 5:22-23).

### Obeying Christ's Commandments

The continual manifestation of the Holy Spirit's filling in one's life is dependent on the person's continually doing the will of God. If we keep Christ's commandments, He promises to manifest Himself to us (John 14:21). Obedience is proof that we love God (I John 5:1-3). Keeping Christ's commandments is not putting ourselves back under the law in order to gain righteousness and favor with God (John 1:17). Christ, at salvation, becomes our righteousness (I Corinthians 1:30). We are under God's grace and look to the Holy Spirit to lead us in obedience to Christ's commandments (Romans 8:14). To us who are under grace, Christ gave only two commandments, faith and love (I John 3:23). We not only should have faith in Christ, and Him alone, for salvation but we also should walk in the Spirit by faith (II Corinthians 5:7) (see chapter 7).

"And this is his commandment, That we should . . . love one another, as he gave us commandment" (I John 3:23). His love commandment has two concepts, loving God with all of our heart, mind, and soul, and loving others. These two concepts encompass the Ten Commandments (see Appendix C). This is the way to keep in communion with God and abide in Him (I John 3:24).

*Loving Others with a Submissive Spirit*

**Principle 2: Loving others. Since God is love, a passion for God generates a tremendous compassion for others. You, then, become a channel of God's love for people (I John 4:7-8, 18).** It is manifested by submitting one to the other and esteeming others better than self in the various areas of life as given in Ephesians 5:21–6:9. Verses 22-24 urge wives to submit to their husbands, even to non-Christian husbands who meet none of the expectations of wives. First Peter 3:1-6 emphasizes complete submission as long as it does not go against God's commandments (Acts 5:29). In verse 25 of Ephesians 5 husbands are told to lovingly submit to the needs and desires of the wife. The man is told to love his wife as his own body and have the same intimacy with her as he does with Christ (Ephesians 5:26-31). This kind of submission is reemphasized in I Peter 3:7, where the husband is told to understand the wife's weaknesses and give honor unto her. In Ephesians 6:1-3 children are told to submit to their parents. In verse 4 fathers are told to submit to the growing needs of their children by training them in the nurture and admonition of the Lord. In Ephesians 6:5-8 hired servants are commanded to submit to their superiors, doing them service with love, even to masters who are mean and cruel (I Peter 2:18). Employers are to submit to the needs of the employees, treating them well with love (Ephesians 6:9). All Christians are to submit to duly constituted government and authority (I Peter 2:13-17). However, it is extremely hard for a Christian to submit to others when he has not first submitted his life to the full control of the Holy Spirit. A proud spirit, arrogance, or the lack of a servant's heart is a sure sign of failure to submit to God's control.

### *Loving Others with a Servant Attitude*

Essential to loving others effectively is a servant attitude. Jesus gave the pattern by washing the disciples' feet (John 13:15). If any would be the greatest, he needs to put himself last and become a servant (Mark 9:35). Jesus took upon Himself the form of a servant when He was made in the likeness of man and became obedient unto death, and we are to be of the same mind (Philippians 2:5-8). We are told to be clothed with humility, for God resists the proud and gives grace to the humble (I Peter 5:5-6).

In the Roman Empire, slavery was an accepted part of life. The Roman legions would bring back the conquered Arabs and Europeans and sell them to the wealthy as bond slaves to be owned by a master and under his complete control. Servanthood was well known to the people Jesus addressed.

All Christians are called to be willing bond slaves of Christ, for all are bought with a price (I Corinthians 6:20). To become a bond slave of Christ, a person must make a decision to surrender his body with its self-orientation (flesh) and present it to Christ as a living sacrifice (Romans 12:1-2; Galatians 2:20). This is a total commitment to follow God's will wherever He leads and do whatever He requires (Matthew 10:37-39; 16:24-25). It is a vow to daily trust Christ to work in and through one instead of working for Him (Philippians 2:13; I Thessalonians 5:24). For some Christians this dedication decision is made at salvation, but most Christian's make it at a later time. (See chapter 3, step 2, of How to Be Filled with the Holy Spirit.)

The result of being a bond slave of Christ is a life of servanthood dedicated to serving and loving Christ and others instead of self. To have the heart of a bond slave to Christ is to have the mind of a servant who serves others. Even though one voluntarily becomes a bondservant and submits to Christ's complete control, he still enjoys the love, blessing, and privileges of sonship and friendship with Christ (I John 3:1-3; John

15:14-15). Paul referred to himself as a servant of Jesus Christ in Romans 1:1, Philippians 1:1, and Titus 1:1. He also called Timothy and Epaphras servants (Colossians 4:12; Philippians 1:1). James and Jude, half brothers of Christ, Peter, and John all called themselves servants of Christ (James 1:1; Jude 1; II Peter 1:1; Revelation 1:1). The word "servant" in the original Greek, as used in the above passages, refers to being a bond slave and is used only once referring to Christ as a bondservant (Philippians 2:7). He divested Himself of all but His deity and humbly served the Father by dying on the cross for the sins of mankind in obedience to the will of His Father. If we are to have the mind of Christ, we must become bond slaves of Christ and take on the role of servants.

In Matthew 7:13-18 and 6:19-34, Jesus teaches about two roads. One is the broad road leading to eternal punishment without God, and one is the narrow road leading to eternal life with God. Everyone starts on the broad road at birth, and sometime before death one must choose to enter in the straight gate of salvation by receiving Jesus Christ as Lord and Savior and follow the narrow road leading to everlasting life. While on this road the Christian chooses to dedicate himself to be a bond slave who loves and serves Christ and others.

Progress on the broad road leading to destruction is motivated by love of money, which buys possessions, power, prestige, and popularity and elevates self. When the sinner arrives at the time of death, he leaves this temporary trash behind, for all mankind come into the world with nothing, and all leave the world with nothing (Ecclesiastes 2; I Timothy 6:7). Advancement on the narrow road is motivated by love for God and His righteousness and enthrones Christ. On this road, God gives a desire to the Christian to magnify, glorify, and proclaim the name of Christ through servanthood by giving instead of taking and thus laying up treasures in heaven. The Christian's fulfillment never comes from self-gratification. Success and exaltation in God's economy come only through servanthood (Matthew 20:26-28).

### Characteristics of Servants

If we were to profile a servant of Christ biblically, the following seven characteristics would emerge:

1. Love (I John 3:16-17). Servants of Christ love God with all their heart, mind, and soul because God first loved them. God puts a love in their hearts for others, which is manifested by serving others. They are courteous, tenderhearted, and forgiving and have wisdom to control the tongue. They have compassion for the suffering, tragedy, and needs of others.

2. Submission (Romans 13:1-6). Servants of Christ have a spirit of meekness, submission, and obedience to the authority that God has placed over them. Their submission and obedience never conflicts with the Word of God. They are not guilty or resisting, griping, or rebelling against authority.

3. Humility (Philippians 2:3-4). Servants of Christ humbly serve, esteeming others better than themselves and rarely thinking of self. They respect and listen to the ideas and suggestions of others. They do not serve to gain favor, recognition, or exaltation of men. They know that God resists the proud and gives grace to the humble. They are also aware that they will be "lifted up" if they humble themselves.

4. Generosity (II Corinthians 9:5-8). Servants of Christ are alert to the needs of others and respond by giving time, energy, money, and possessions to meet the needs of others. They claim no rightful ownership of anything, realizing that they are merely stewards of God's property and assets. Even their homes, which most use as a place of privacy and

retreat, they open to strangers, both sinners and saints. Servants use their homes as places to win the lost and edify the saints by having Bible studies, showing Christian videos, and entertaining others. Their goal is to build relationships.

5. Trust (Proverbs 3:5-6). Servants of Christ face suffering, adversity, and disappointment with a positive faith attitude and give thanks. They do not react to adverse situations with self pity, complaints, or questions such as "why me?" and "why now?" They trust God for the grace and strength to handle any situation. They trust God always to meet their needs and to supply the wherewithal to meet the needs of others.

6. Encouragement (Ephesians 4:29). Servants of Christ are ready to give a good word fitly spoken to encourage and to edify others. They are careful about conversation or actions that would tear down or humiliate others. They are sensitive to the feelings, perceptions, and expectations of others.

7. Obedience (John 14:21). Servants of Christ are excited and fervent about spreading the gospel and Bible principles worldwide and loving others in response to Christ's command. They are obedient to the will of God as revealed in the Scripture and to the leading of the Holy Spirit. They access the power of the Holy Spirit by daily prayer. The following table shows the contrasts between servants of Christ and servants of self.

*Table 2*

**Servant Characteristics**

|  | *Servants of Christ* | *Servants of Self* |
|---|---|---|
| *Love* | Walk in love serving others (I John 2:6). | Walk in indifference, fear, and anger that often leads to bitterness and seeking vengeance (Ephesians 4:31). |
| *Submission* | Have a spirit of submission and obedience to authority (I Timothy 6:1-2). | Resist, rebel, and gripe against authority (Romans 13:2). |
| *Humility* | Humbly serve with singleness of heart and good will as unto Christ (Ephesians 6:5-7). | Serve to please men, to gain favor and recognition (Ephesians 6:6). |
| *Generosity* | Respond with compassion to meet the needs of others (I John 3:18). | Ignore or disregard the needs of others (I John 3:17). |
| *Trust* | Face suffering, adversity, and disappointment with a positive faith attitude and give thanks (I Thessalonians 5:18). | React to adverse situations with self pity, complaints, and questions (Ephesians 4:17-19). |
| *Encouragement* | Search for opportunities to encourage, to serve, and to do good (Matthew 25:35-40). | Selfishly expect encouragement and service from others (Matthew 25:41-46). |
| *Obedience* | Show excitement and fervency about spreading the gospel and Christ's teachings and Bible principles worldwide (Matthew 28:19-20). | Reject the gospel demands and commands of Christ (I Corinthians 15:34). |

A third grade teacher in Minnesota devised a unique way to effectively implement one of these characteristics of Christian servanthood. To encourage her students, she had them list the names of their classmates, leaving a space under each name. She then had them write a sentence describing the nicest thing about each classmate. The teacher worked on her own list. On the weekend the teacher compiled the encouraging words from each list for each child and added her own comments to each list. This was the child's private list to read when he needed encouragement.

*Listening to God*

Being obedient to God with a servant attitude necessitates listening to God by being sensitive to the prompting of the Holy Spirit about what to do and say to others and when to do it. A good word fitly spoken, a meal taken to a sick neighbor, a timely twenty dollar bill given in an emergency, a note or telephone call of encouragement, and help given to a stranded motorist are examples of Spirit-led deeds. These deeds of love not only tangibly reveal and glorify God but also open witnessing opportunities that may produce eternal results. Needs are often revealed when we listen carefully to the replies to our habitual probing questions such as "How are things going?" or "Can I be of help?"

## Maintaining a Spirit-filled Life

Greek scholars agree that the verb in Ephesians 5:18 that commands us to be filled with the Spirit is a present imperative. This implies that the Christian is to leave his life open to be filled repeatedly by the divine Spirit's power and control. Regeneration, or the indwelling of the Holy Spirit, is a once for all, never to be repeated experience. The filling of the Spirit is an initial experience at dedication, but every time you are motivated by the flesh and give into the self life, you commit sin. It is then necessary to confess the sin and let the Holy Spirit fill you anew and take control. That is why we are admonished by Christ to deny self and take up our cross daily and follow Him (Luke 9:23).

The rebound principle is important to maintaining a Spirit-filled life.

*Table 3*

**The Rebound Principle**

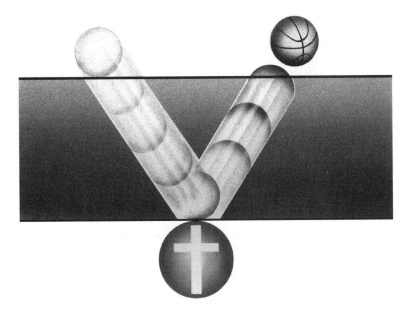

When we sin, we fall down to the carnal level. The longer we stay on this level the farther we get from the Spirit-filled life. Once one sins and hits the carnal level, he needs to rebound right away by confessing the sin and to bounce back to the spiritual level (I John 1:9). The barrier at the end of the carnal level in Table 3 is our blessed assurance that we will not lose the indwelling Holy Spirit (John 10:28-29). Sin is like a heavy black cloud cover in a winter storm, blocking and dimming the light, power, and warmth of the sun. Repentance and confession cause the wind of God's forgiveness to remove clouds of sin and allow the sunlight of God's love to shine in full power again, warming the soul (I John 1:7-9). Sin starts in the mind with wicked, lustful thoughts and devilish imaginations (James 1:14-15). To have victory over sin and walk in the Spirit, a Christian must cast out imaginations and think Christ's thoughts (II Corinthians 10:5; Philippians 4:8).

Victory over sin also involves avoiding the philosophy and influence of the world (I John 2:15-16). Personal holiness demands biblical standards governing the lifestyle of the believer, especially in the area of entertainment and predominantly in television programs and professional sports. Worldly entertainment poses a grave danger to the Spirit-filled Christian, for it consumes a great deal of time and attention, corrupts and trivializes moral character, serves as a refuge from a troubled conscience, and may eventually become a god that displaces Jehovah God.

*Body-Temple Principle*

The Bible declares that our bodies are the temple of the Holy Spirit (I Corinthians 3:16; 6:19-20). Figuratively speaking, there are four doors to this temple: (1) The world door, opening to the lust of the eyes and pride, (2) the flesh door, opening to corrupt desires, (3) the faith door, opening to God's love and grace, (4) the love door, opening to our ministry of care and compassion to others (Table 4). Once we become born-again, the first two doors should remain closed. The latter two doors should remain wide open. We are warned to not love the world or the things in the world (I John 2:15-16). We are instructed to walk in the Spirit so that we will not fulfill the desires of the flesh (Galatians 5:16). The door of faith is open when we believe on Christ as our Savior. We need to put our complete trust in Him in all areas and circumstances of life. We should thank Him for all things, for we know that it is His will and that he works all things for our good (I Thessalonians 5:18; Romans 8:28). God pours His love into our lives for His glory. We ought to keep the love door wide open and be a channel of His love to others, reaching and serving others. The Holy Spirit, filling our lives, gives us power to serve. We dare not shut the door of faith or we will lack the love and power to reach others effectively and to bear spiritual fruit. If we close the door of love to others, we become selfish and self-centered, and we will grieve and quench the Spirit. The Spirit-filled walk keeps the inflow door of faith open and the outflow door of love open, thereby serving as an open channel of God's love and grace. This is the way to have the power of the Spirit to be able to use our gifts to the glory of God in the ministry that God has given to us.

*Table 4*

### Body—Temple of the Holy Spirit

## Summary

A willing Spirit-filled walk that promotes holiness must increase and abound in love for God and others. "And the Lord make you to increase and abound in love one toward another, and toward all men, even as we do toward you: To the end he may stablish your hearts unblameable in holiness before God, even our Father, at the coming of our Lord Jesus Christ with all his saints" (I Thessalonians 3:12-13).

A love for God results in love and compassion for people exhibited through servanthood. We serve and glorify God by serving people. The Holy Spirit's filling us not only gives us the desire to serve God and others but gives us the grace and guidance to help needy people. They may be in need of the gospel, spiritual counseling, encouragement, and physical or material help.

The Spirit-filled Christian is sensitive to the Holy Spirit's guidance by discerning and responding appropriately. Unfeigned love and obedience is the key to walking with God.

Chapter 5

# THE WORTHY SPIRIT-FILLED WALK THAT PROMOTES UNITY IN THE CHURCH

PHASE 3

God in His embracing love cares about our individual lives, our needs, and our concerns. He is equally concerned with our relationships and interactions with other believers in His body, the church. Jesus put great emphasis on how we act and react with other Christians and on the love and concern we have for them.

### *Jesus' Teaching on Unity*

In John 17, after His extensive teaching in chapters 14-16 on the subject of the ministry of the Holy Spirit in the lives of the believers, Jesus, in His prayer to the Father, stresses the importance of the believers' unity with each other. Even at this last gathering with the disciples before His crucifixion, He has observed that they came to the supper with Him in a spirit of seeking to gain the best places for themselves. He is therefore concerned that any future work they might attempt will be hindered by disunity. In verses 1-8, He speaks of the foundation for their unity—His own deity, the salvation which He came to bring, and the teachings He had given them to obey—and then earnestly prays for their unity.

In verses 14-19, He again stresses the foundation upon which this unity is to be built, THE TRUTH. Then he returns to the subject of the task that they are to undertake in His name. The Holy Spirit guides the walk of the Spirit-filled Christian in the body of believers to bring about the unity Jesus emphasizes.

### Biblical Unity

True biblical unity in the spiritual body of Christ and the local church is centered on the foundation of Christ's virgin birth, blood atonement, and resurrection. That is the heart of the gospel made available to individuals *only* by God's grace working through the Holy Spirit and received *only* by faith.

In the second half of the twentieth century, Christian leaders sought to unify Christians on a number of unstable foundations, including ecumenical evangelism, prayer for worldwide revival, speaking in tongues, conservative political action, contemporary music, and a family emphasis focusing on responsible fatherhood and committed motherhood. These shaky foundations for unity were sincerely promoted in a spurious attempt to make the gospel less threatening and more relevant and to exhibit toleration for diverse beliefs.

Spiritual unity centered on any other foundation than Christ's virgin birth, atonement, and resurrection, no matter how laudable, causes diminished scriptural authority, confused Christians, and damnation of souls if it leads people to trust in their false beliefs for salvation.

God desires, honors, and blesses unity among the brethren. Christians should always work toward unity within the framework of the Word of God if they want to be led of the Spirit, serve the Lord effectively, and do God's will. Psalm 133:1 indicates that it is very pleasant "for brethren to dwell together in unity." And verse 3 says that the Lord will commend His blessing to those who come together in unity. To dwell in unity with others, one must first have a heart to fear the Lord. That means that he must not harbor sin in his life, especially the sins of bitterness, hatred, and malice. Sin shatters the unity and the fellowship of the saints. It also hinders fellowship with God (I John 1:5-9). Love is a cohesive factor that binds Christians together in unity and fellowship. Christians are taught of God to love one another: "But as touching brotherly love ye need not that I write unto you: for ye yourselves are taught of God to love one another" (I Thessalonians 4:9). As one increases in love, his heart is established "unblameable in holiness before God" (I Thessalonians 3:12-13). Anything that works against this love is sin.

First Corinthians 1:9-10 indicates that unity is God's desire for Christian brethren and the church. The same idea is given in Philippians 2:2-5: Christians should "be likeminded, having the same love, being of one accord, of one mind" (v. 2). This like-mindedness is best accomplished by the admonition in verses 3-5: "Let nothing be done through strife or vainglory; but in lowliness of mind let each esteem other better than themselves. Look not every man on his own things, but every man also on the things of others. Let this mind be in you, which was also in Christ Jesus."

The Book of Ephesians details God's desire for unity; Ephesians 1:10 says that eventually, in the fullness of time, God wants to "gather together in one all things in Christ." At salvation, He has "quickened us together with Christ . . . and hath raised us up together, and made us sit together in heavenly places" (Ephesians 2:5-6), and the Christian can experience this full identification with Christ by daily living the crucified life (Luke 9:23). Christ has broken down the middle wall of partition between Jew and Gentile and God and man through His blood so that all men can be reconciled to God (Ephesians 2:13-16). We are now made fellow citizens with the saints in the household of God (Ephesians 2:19, 22). He then calls for Christians to forbear one another in love so that there will be a unity within the body of Christ (Ephesians 4:2-6). In the unity of faith, the body is properly joined together and edifies itself in love (Ephesians 4:13, 16). The ultimate example of human unity is the one-flesh unity between the husband and wife in marriage (Ephesians 5:31-33).

*Biblical Separation*

Spiritual unity is built upon the foundation of Christ Himself (I Corinthians 3:11). It is apparent in the Scriptures that when the clear teachings of the Word of God are violated, there are justifiable reasons for division and separation of brethren from each other. Proper biblical unity in the body of Christ involves separation from unbelievers (II Corinthians 6:14-17). To preserve in the church the holiness of God and the integrity of the Scriptures, Christians are not to be joined together with unbelievers in any union, either religious or secular, in which the unbelievers can have control to affect the Christian's doctrine or testimony (II John 9-11). Separation from believers should occur only when the believers are disorderly (II Thessalonians 3:6, 14-15; I Timothy 6:3, 5), when the believers are disobedient, walking in the flesh (I Corinthians 5:11), and when they transgress and refuse to be disciplined by the church (Matthew 18:15-17). Most disunity, however, has nothing to do with purity of doctrine or the purity of the church in these other areas. Rather, it has to do with conflicts between personalities; loyalty to men and false teachers rather than God; selfish ambitions and desires; jealousy and bitterness;

an unforgiving spirit among believers; and selfish, uncaring, and unloving hearts.

*A Worthy Walk*

There are many passages dealing with the subject of the Spirit-filled Christian's walk in the church, including Romans 14 and 15 and I Corinthians 8-10; but the most direct teaching on the subject is found in Ephesians 4. This book relates to the walk of the Spirit-filled Christian in the local church. Paul introduces chapter 4 of Ephesians by speaking of the worthiness of our walk before the Lord (4:1). This is essential if we are to be approved by Him and He is to be satisfied and happy with our lives. The proof of this worthy Spirit-filled walk is our ministry to other believers. Paul speaks of their need to have a meek spirit toward each other, which manifests itself in their love, long-suffering, and forbearance to bring unity in the church (4:2-3). All of the illustrations given in Ephesians 4:4-7 emphasize that nothing from God is divided and, therefore, God's church is not to be divided. When we create disunity, we are out of the will of God and cannot expect His blessing. In Ephesians 4:7-16, the emphasis is on the gifts of leadership. The passage shows not only that the Holy Spirit raises up these leaders but also that one of the main purposes for their ministry is to bring about unity in the local church.

*Achieving Unity in Relationships*

To bring about the unity mentioned in Ephesians 4:13, the Spirit-filled Christian will make up his Spirit-filled mind (v. 23) to put off the corrupt old man's habitual behaviors (v. 22) and put on the biblical new man's habitual behaviors (v. 24), rightfully called disciplines of grace (Table 5). Some of these behaviors are as follows:

*Table 5*

**Disciplines of Grace**

(Ephesians 4:1-32)

|  | *Put Off* | *Put On* |
|---|---|---|
| 4:2 | Pride and intolerance causing disunity. | Meekness and forebearance keeping peaceful unity of the Spirit (4:2-3) |
| 4:14 | Immaturity by following false teaching | Maturity by seeking and speaking the truth in love (4:15) |
| 4:18 | A mind alienated from God through ignorance and blindness to God's ways | Learning from Jesus and His Word (4:20) |
| 4:19 | Uncleanness with greediness | Righteousness and true holiness (4:24) |
| 4:25 | Lying | Speaking truth (4:25) |
| 4:26 | Unrestrained anger | Resolving anger before sunset (4:26) |
| 4:28 | Stealing | Working to have and share (4:28) |
| 4:29 | Corrupt conversation | Conversation that edifies (4:29) |
| 4:31 | Bitterness, wrath, clamor, and malice | Kindness, tenderheartedness, and forgiveness (4:32) |

These "put ons," or acquired characteristics (disciplines of grace), of a Spirit-filled Christian are the marks of a spiritual person (Galatians 5:22-23). The Holy Spirit gives the enabling power to make these virtues a habitual part of daily behavior. The feeling-motivated habits of sin oriented toward self must be replaced by the mind-motivated habits of holiness oriented toward

Christlikeness. This replacement can be accomplished only in the power of the Spirit as He works through the Christian's daily intake of the Word of God. The Spirit-filled Christian must practice the habits of holiness. It usually takes about six weeks for a new habit pattern to become an automatic response.

### The Sin of Bitterness

Unresolved anger with a desire for revenge, which results in bitterness, is probably the most common sin of Christians who cause disunity in the church. It usually starts in families and spills over into the church, disrupting a climate of love and defiling many Christians. Bitterness with a desire for vengeance is like a weak thread in a beautiful tapestry of Christian unity. When a break occurs in our relationship, we try to patch it up instead of getting rid of the root of bitterness that defiles many people (Hebrews 12:15). Bitterness is most commonly displayed by conversation. When one feels continual anger about a situation, toward an individual who has violated his imagined rights, or even toward God, his memory goes into action every time the person or situation is mentioned and adds fuel to the fires of past unpleasant experiences. Bitterness handcuffs one to a perceived enemy. Plotting and planning revenge keeps the person from using the key of forgiveness, which would bring freedom. Confession and a forgiving spirit, which involves giving up a desire to get revenge, are the only remedies for bitterness. They are also the only ways to restore the unity that God wants.

### A Spiritual Testimony

To have a worthy walk, a Spirit-filled Christian will make up his mind to put off sinful actions and put on godly behavior. He will let the Holy Spirit work in and through him, manifesting Christ's love and forgiveness in all his relationships because he is a worker with Christ. He is not to receive the grace of God in vain or give offense in anything by ungodly conduct (II Corinthians

6:1-3). In Titus 2, Christians are told to live holy lives lest the Word of God be blasphemed (2:5) so that those who oppose them may be ashamed (2:8) and so that they may adorn the doctrine of God, the Savior, in all things (2:10). God's grace teaches believers and provides the power by the Holy Spirit to put off ungodliness and worldly lusts (2:11-12). Grace also teaches and gives power to "live soberly," putting on a biblical lifestyle, to "live righteously," by showing love to others by our good works, and to "live godly," by worshiping and praising God with a life lived to His glory in the present world (2:12). God uses divine discipline to bring about the changes to conform believers to Christlikeness (Hebrews 12:5-14). Christians then have the confidence to look for the blessed hope (Titus 2:13-14).

These godly habits of behavior, or disciplines of grace, make the worthy walk of the Spirit-filled Christian a daily revelation of the character of Jesus Christ, bring unity in the church, and pave the way for a gospel witness to unbelievers.

Chapter 6

# THE WITNESSING SPIRIT-FILLED WALK THAT PRODUCES SPIRITUAL FRUIT

The Holy Spirit manifests His power by implanting in the Spirit-filled believer a strong desire to develop the two distinguishing attributes of a Spirit-filled Christian life. (1) Obedience, by transforming his mind and will from the self-controlled flesh life to the Christ-controlled faith life. This is accomplished by deciding to abide in Christ. (2) Loving others by using the gifts that God has given to reach others with the gospel, to disciple, and to edify the saints, which produces lasting spiritual fruit.

### Abiding in Christ

Abiding in Christ is essential to the Christ-controlled faith life that reaches others and bears eternal fruit. Jesus said, "I am the true vine, and my Father is the husbandman. Every branch in me that beareth not fruit he taketh away: and every branch that beareth fruit, he purgeth it, that it may bring forth more fruit. Now ye are clean through the word which I have spoken unto you. Abide in me, and I in you. As the branch cannot bear fruit of itself, except it abide in the vine; no more can ye, except ye abide in me. I am the vine, ye are the branches: He that abideth in me, and I in him, the same bringeth forth much fruit: for without me ye can do nothing. . . . Ye have not chosen me, but I have chosen you, and ordained you, that ye should go and bring forth fruit, and that your fruit should remain: that whatsoever ye shall ask of the Father in my name, he may give it you" (John 15:1-5, 16). Jesus is not only the author of our faith but also the finisher of our faith (Hebrews 12:2). For our salvation we are looking to Jesus by faith, and for a fruitful life of service we are looking to Jesus continually by faith.

To abide in Christ, a believer must firmly comprehend two important spiritual truths. (1) The flesh, or self, produces dead works before and after salvation. Even after salvation the believer's flesh is incapable of producing spiritual fruit. (2) Spiritual life is only in Christ, and the only way to transmit this life to others is to abide in Christ and depend on the power of His Spirit. The way to have the power to produce eternal fruit is to abide in, to depend on, and to look to Jesus Christ, who lives within the believer, manifested through the Holy Spirit (John 15:16). Jesus compared this relationship to a branch, which depends on the vine for life (John 15:4-5). Other comparisons can be made: the shining moon depends on the sun to reflect its light, the bubbling fountain depends on the reservoir for water, and the complex computer depends on electricity for power. If we are going to reflect the light for the world, to give the water of life to sinners, or to have any power in our ministry, we must abide in Christ by depending on the Holy Spirit to manifest Christ's love and life in and through our lives. We abide in Christ in five ways found in Psalm 37: (1) "Trust in the Lord" (v. 3), (2) "Delight thyself also in the Lord" (v. 4), (3) "Commit thy way unto the Lord" (v. 5), (4) "Rest in the Lord" (v. 7), (5) "Wait patiently for him" (v. 7). We can best follow these commands by daily taking time to read and meditate on Scripture and to worship God with our prayers of adoration, praise, and thanksgiving.

*Power for a Gospel Ministry*

A Spirit-filled Christian has an overwhelming desire to fulfill the ministry that God has assigned to him, and by abiding in Christ he will produce spiritual fruit. A spiritual gospel ministry might be defined as letting God use gifts that He has given us to work in and through us to evangelize and edify others for His glory.

Pentecost was a fulfillment of Old Testament prophecy about the coming of the Holy Spirit. When Jesus gave the Great Commission to the disciples, He told them to wait in Jerusalem for the coming of the Holy Spirit. When the Holy Spirit came, they would become Christ's witnesses in Jerusalem, Judea, Samaria, and to the ends of the earth; through the coming of the Holy Spirit at Pentecost, the power was given to the apostles to be witnesses of the gospel of Christ. The whole book of Acts is an elaboration of the theme of witnessing.

The manner in which the Holy Spirit came illustrates the crucial role He was to play in the lives and ministries of the apostles and all believers. The wind signifies the power, the fire signifies the purifying effect of His presence, and the tongues signify the preaching of the gospel in all languages to all nations. All point to the Holy Spirit's ministry to the believer, enabling him to reach others with the love of Christ. The main ministry of the Holy Spirit is to reveal the mystery of Christ, "which is Christ in you, the hope of glory" (Colossians 1:27). Christ's life and love are imparted by the Holy Spirit to the unbeliever when he responds to the proclaimed Word of God (the gospel) by repenting and believing in Christ.

This was the significant reason for Pentecost, for the Holy Spirit to give the gifts and the power to the believers that make up the church to enable them to proclaim and reach the world with the gospel.

*Motivation for a Gospel Ministry*

Jesus described His earthly mission as a "seek and save" ministry or, as some people have called it, a "search and rescue" mission. Luke 19:10 states, "For the Son of man is come to seek and to save that which was lost." Jesus in Luke 15 had used parables common to the culture of His day to illustrate the urgency of seeking the lost. He used the "lost sheep" and the "lost coin" parables to stress the importance of the mission. Today hundreds of people will turn out to find a lost child, a lost hiker, or a missing person because they are afraid of the fate that will befall the individual. The Spirit-filled Christian, in his love for others, realizes the fate that will befall a sinner. "It is appointed unto men once to die, but after this the judgment" (Hebrews 9:27). We get a glimpse of the severity of the terrible judgment in II Thessalonians 1:7-9. The certain judgment of God awaits the sinner. Christ is his only salvation, and that fact is a motivation for our constant engagement in evangelism. "Knowing therefore the terror of the Lord, we persuade men" (II Corinthians 5:11). The Spirit-filled Christian, abiding in Christ, has another motivation, found in II Corinthians 5:14, "For the love of Christ constraineth us." He lets the love of Christ flow through him to others, giving him a new attitude toward sinners. He sees them as they really are—people lost and going to hell rather than people to be emulated in lifestyle, dress, and corrupt behavior. Our zeal in declaring the gospel to the condemned sinner depends on the value we place on Christ's sacrifice on the cross for lost sinners and on His resurrection.

*Phases of a Gospel Ministry*

Evangelism falls into five phases requiring increasing holy boldness, which is found through the power of the Holy Spirit.

Phase 1 is the simple act of inviting people out to church or some gospel service. Several large churches have taken surveys of the souls that were saved in their church services and found that most of the new converts (87 percent in one study) were visitors who had been invited by church members.

The Sunday school or Christian school teacher can encourage his students to invite their unsaved friends or family members to a gospel service at church, youth meetings, or an evangelistic rally. Check up once a week to see how many are inviting someone to a gospel service.

Phase 2 in soulwinning is to start carrying and giving out tracts. This is a more difficult and bolder witness. Make an agreement with the Lord to pass out at least one or two tracts every single week, personally giving the tract to a friend or somebody you meet. Studies have shown that about one of every hundred Christians was converted as a result of reading a tract.

A modern-day version of tracts is appealing cards advertising a gospel-proclaiming website. A teacher can organize a tract blitz on Saturday to cover the whole town or a section of a city with gospel tracts and information about a fundamental Bible-believing church. The students can also pass out tracts to public school students outside of the school grounds.

Phase 3 of soulwinning is giving a gospel testimony directly to others. Whenever one is alone with a person for any length of time, he should present the claims of Christ. This phase is a little more difficult, for it requires some holy boldness. In this phase the soulwinner talks to a person and gives testimony of his salvation, reading aloud or quoting the verses that people used to lead him to Christ, telling how he reacted, what he thought, and what he did about it. These personal testimonies of salvation can be a powerful influence on unsaved people. A teacher can ask students to give testimonies about gospel contacts and responses during the past week.

Phase 4 is getting a target individual, a friend, relative, or new acquaintance, winning him to the Lord Jesus Christ, and then discipling him. In a Church Growth, Inc., survey of forty-two thousand lay people who came to Christ, 75-90 percent of them became Christians through the witness of friends or relatives. At most, only 2 percent were won by visitation programs, less than 1 percent were won through evangelistic crusades or television programs, and just 6 percent credited church programs with bringing them to faith in Christ. The phase starts by a person's inviting and taking an unsaved person to Sunday school, church services, gospel meetings, and activities. It continues as he gives a personal witness whenever possible and even goes to the point of fasting and praying for the target individual (who may be a friend or loved one). It may include inviting him over for a meal and playing an audio or video Christian testimony of a well-known personality or showing a gospel video. Once that person has been led to Jesus Christ, the friend sets out to disciple him. In this way he becomes a II Timothy 2:2 discipler, something few people in the church ever achieve. The discipler is a Spirit-controlled believer who helps a new or weaker Christian to acquire and live the principles and promises of God's Word with the goal of knowing and becoming like Christ. Christlike love and servanthood must be the ongoing goal of every Christian (Philippians 2:5-11).

The discipler urges the new convert to be baptized, to join a Bible-believing church, and to have a regular Bible study with him. Becoming a real friend, the discipler takes the new believer to church and soulwinning, encourages him to memorize verses, and does everything he can to build him up in the faith. One survey of 240 new Christians and 240 "dropouts" revealed that 94 percent of the active believers stayed in the church because of their friendship with the person who witnessed to them. On the other hand, 71 percent of those who dropped out did so because they viewed the evangelist as a salesman, not a friend. A teacher can encourage individual students to pick out a friend or relative as their target and have them give weekly reports of their witnessing opportunities so that the whole class can pray for the targeted individuals.

Phase 5 is becoming involved in some gospel ministry, such as testifying or preaching in a jail service, a rescue mission service, or a street meeting, teaching Sunday school classes, working on a bus route, holding child evangelism clubs in the neighborhood, or going on a mission team. The Christian participating in these soulwinning activities is more open to the Holy Spirit's call to full-time Christian service.

The teacher can organize and lead a mission team in conjunction with a church youth group. With his students' help, he can also hold a Bible club for public school students one evening every week. He might want to set in place the policy that Christian school students may attend only if they bring a public school student. In the church or Christian school, the teacher can start a soulwinners' club for students who have made a commitment to serve the Lord as a missionary, pastor, evangelist, or Christian school teacher or to go into any other type of Christian service. This club can meet on campus before or after school and attract other interested students.

The approach to the unbeliever in soulwinning should always be twofold, as alluded to in Jude 22-23. "And of some have compassion [mercy], making a difference." Some people respond better to the love of God and to a loving, tender approach. Others need a more confrontational approach, a warning of judgment and the wrath of God against sin: "And others save with fear, pulling them out of the fire; hating even the garment spotted by the flesh." Both approaches should be used with every unbeliever, but one will receive more emphasis than the other, depending on the person and his reaction.

*The Techniques*

The techniques of evangelism are many and varied, but the gospel message is always the same for dealing with the lost. The technique the soulwinner uses will depend on his personality and the situation. There are many people who are hungry for the gospel, and a soulwinner trusts the Holy Spirit to lead him to the hungry ones. The Spirit-filled Christian is always ready to give out the "gospel sandwich" to satisfy the hunger of lost sinners.

The bottom piece of bread in this "gospel sandwich" is a friendly spirit, getting acquainted and being interested in the lost person. It would also include a question inquiring about his spiritual condition, such as "If you were to die right now, would you go to heaven or hell?" or "Could you tell me in a few words how a person could be sure of going to heaven?"

The meat of the "gospel sandwich" is six to ten verses explaining salvation, such as Romans 3:23; 6:23; 5:8; 10:9-13; Hebrews 9:27; II Thessalonians 1:7-9; Ephesians 2:8-9; John 1:12; and I John 5:11-13. (See Appendix B.) The word "sin" in Romans 3:23 and Romans 6:23 is best explained by going through the Ten Commandments, explaining how the person has broken every one of the Ten Commandments. James 2:10 explains that if anyone has broken one of them, he has broken them all. This approach is important, "for by the law is the knowledge of sin" (Romans 3:19-20; Psalm 19:7-9). The law becomes a teacher to bring us to Christ (Galatians 3:24). A person needs to become desperate for God's salvation. Some people use the Romans Road; others use the third chapter of John. There are many ways to present the gospel, but always the Word of God must be used (Romans 10:17).

The top piece of bread in the "gospel sandwich" is the offer of an opportunity to accept Christ as Savior. This offer is usually in the form of a question, such as "Would you like to receive Christ as your Savior now?" or "In the light of what the Word of God says, what would you like to do about this matter?"

Under no circumstances should a soulwinner promise a sinner an easier life, wealth, or health; for even though he receives eternal life, he may face a life of persecution, suffering, and difficulties ahead. God does say that there will be persecution for all those who live godly in Christ Jesus (II Timothy 3:12). The soulwinner can promise God's eternal love and blessing, the abundant life (John 10:10) with Christ supplying every need (Philippians 4:19), giving grace in every situation (II Corinthians 8:9), and never leaving the person alone in any circumstance (Matthew 28:20; Hebrews 13:5).

One of the most powerful techniques is the soulwinner's personal testimony with appropriate Scriptures of how God brought about his own changed life. This personal testimony must be backed up by a lifestyle of love and holiness so that the unbeliever can see a truly changed life. The witnessing Christian must be led of the Holy Spirit in using the techniques listed above. He has to be totally dependent on the convicting power of the Holy Spirit to apply the powerful word of God to the sinner's soul if he expects repentance and genuine salvation.

*Gospel Truths*

The soulwinner is declaring certain ideas. (1) Man is a sinner, has broken God's law, and needs a Savior because there is terrible judgment coming on sin. (2) Man cannot save himself by his own works or by "turning over a new leaf" or by joining some church. (3) Jesus Christ, God's Son, died on the cross for man's sin, shedding His precious blood as a payment for the sin. (4) Jesus Christ is the resurrected Savior, who has the power to save man from sin because of His resurrection. Sinners must not only believe these truths but must also repent of, or turn from, their sin and receive Jesus Christ into their lives as a personal Savior.

Many times salvation not only saves a person's soul but also clears up a multitude of problems in his life. The Bible details some rewards of successful soulwinning: "Let him know, that he which converteth the sinner from the error of his way shall save a soul from death, and shall hide a multitude of sins" (James 5:20). "And the servant of the Lord must not strive; but be gentle unto all men, apt to teach, patient, in meekness instructing those that oppose themselves; if God peradventure will give them repentance to the acknowledging of the truth; and that they may recover themselves out of the snare of the devil, who are taken captive by him at his will" (II Timothy 2:24-26).

Our high school buddy, Bob Brown, won us to the Lord and wisely motivated us to pursue sinners on the gospel trail. Sixty years later, Bob is still on the gospel trail, having recently won a grade school classmate to the Lord just before she died of cancer (Proverbs 11:30).

A witnessing walk that produces spiritual fruit requires a Spirit-controlled Christian who uses the Word of God to proclaim Jesus Christ as the only way of salvation and trusts in the convicting power of the Holy Spirit to bring sinners to repentance and faith.

Chapter 7

# THE WORD-BASED SPIRIT-FILLED
# FAITH WALK THAT PROMISES VICTORY

PHASE 3

Faith is the critical factor in walking in the Spirit. We began the Christian life by faith in Christ, and we live the Christian life by faith (Romans 1:17). A Spirit-filled willing walk, worthy walk, and witnessing walk can be accomplished only through faith. Faith releases the supernatural power of God to be applied in your life (Matthew 17:20).

### Faith Defined

"Faith is the substance of things hoped for, the evidence of things not seen" (Hebrews 11:1). As A. W. Tozer emphasized in his book *The Knowledge of the Holy*, faith is not imagination but rests on a foundation of real objective truths. Imagination projects unreal images from the mind and makes them seem real. The Christian faith is based on God's revealed truth found in the Bible and in God's creation. The Bible truths are confirmed by numerous secular historical accounts, dating back thousands of years. Archeological discoveries and valid scientific evidence supporting the biblical account of Creation also authenticate the truths. However, the Word of God needs no defense and is understood only by someone who believes in and has a relationship by faith with Jesus Christ as Savior (I Corinthians

2:14). Walking by faith is simply believing God's promises and trusting that God will honor His promises by fulfilling them (Romans 4:21). Good works (the expression of love) are the result and overflow of a vibrant faith. If good works are not evident, faith is nonexistent or dead (James 2:17).

### *Faith That Grows and Flourishes*

For faith to grow and flourish, three things are necessary: (1) To know about the God we worship and serve, (2) to know the Bible principles about faith, (3) to know and believe God's promises about our eternal salvation and every area of our lives.

Abraham was a good example of a man who fully trusted and followed God in obedience and allowed Him to direct his life. Scripture records that although Abraham made a few wrong decisions and had to suffer the consequences, he kept his faith and trust in God and His promises. Because of Abraham's faith in God's promise, God forgave his sins and accepted him as righteous and just. As it was with Abraham, so it is with us. We accept God's promise of eternal life by our faith in Christ's blood atonement and resurrection. We are then declared righteous and just by God for all eternity (Romans 4:20–5:2).

### *A Biblical View of God*

Knowing about the God we worship and serve is the foundation of faith. The more you know God, the greater will be your confidence and trust in Him. Listed below are key life-guiding truths about God that will influence choices of your life purposes, goals, and actions.

*Table 6*

**Life-Guiding Truths About God**

|  | *God Has* | *By Faith We Can Choose To* |
|---|---|---|
| 1. | Perfect love (Isaiah 40:10-11; I John 4:8-10) | Receive it and share |
| 2. | Infinite wisdom (Isaiah 55:8-9; Romans 11:33-34) | Recognize it and submit |
| 3. | Complete control (Daniel 4:17, 35; Ephesians 1:11) | Trust it and rest |
| 4. | Ultimate holiness (Psalm 99:9; I Peter 1:13-16) | Live it and reap |
| 5. | Unlimited creativeness (Psalm 19:1-3; Acts 17:24-25) | Enjoy it and praise |
| 6. | Majestic power (Job 37:10-13; Ephesians 3:20) | Claim it and glorify |

1. God's perfect and all-embracing love was demonstrated ultimately on the cross and confirmed personally at the moment of our salvation. When God comes into our lives, His love strengthens us and does what finally is best for us. We evaluate God's love for us not by our own circumstance but by Christ's death on the cross and His resurrection. We can choose to receive God's love and share and declare it to others.

2. God shows His infinite, reliable wisdom by directing our lives. He guides through His Word and also uses circumstances, church people, and others to reveal His will

to us. He is the light and leads our steps as we walk down the dark path of life. We can choose to recognize His wisdom and submit our will to His.

3. God has absolute, complete control over His creation and all the events of history. All future events are in His absolute control. God is going to fulfill His will and purpose in our lives and in the world. We can choose to trust His control of our life and rest in the knowledge that His will is best for us.

4. God has ultimate, supreme holiness and desires His holiness in our lives. We can choose to live a holy life and reap the benefits of obedience to His Word.

5. God has unlimited, wondrous creativeness, which manifests His glory. It is our human tendency to get so involved in studying details of the natural and physical sciences that we miss the magnificent beauty and grandeur of God's creation, which reflects His essence. The function of creation is a silent testimony to God's reliability. We can choose to enjoy it without understanding all its facets and give continual praise for His wonderful works unto men.

6. God has majestic, awesome power evident in ordering and controlling the elements of our universe and in His various miracles He reveals to us. He demonstrated His power in creation, His resurrection, and our salvation. He continues to show His power to us in answered prayer and in His victory over sin and death. We can choose by faith to claim His power for our lives and glorify His name for the results.

How you live and worship God reveals what you believe about God (John 4:24).

*An Attitude of Faith*

Walking with God involves developing the right attitude toward basic truths about God. An attitude of disbelief will result in our choosing devilish responses. An attitude of faith will result in godly responses. Attitude is the paintbrush of the mind, coloring every thought, decision, action, and word with light or dark hues. The six important truths about God listed in Table 6, combined with an attitude of faith, will motivate godly responses, leading to righteous behavior.

To grow in faith, you must be aware of the biblical truths of faith. You need faith to insure the eternal destiny of your soul and the temporal direction of your life. God will supply the faith you need through the Holy Spirit's revealing the Word to your heart (Romans 10:17). Some important Bible principles on faith follow.

1. Faith must have an object. The object of faith of a born-again Christian is Jesus Christ and His infallible, inspired Word (Hebrews 12:2).

2. Faith has a motivation. The motivation of faith is hope resulting in a positive attitude (Hebrews 11:1).

3. Faith needs an expression. The expression of faith is love. This is evidenced by good deeds in the Christian's life (Galatians 5:6; James 2:17, 26).

4. Faith is necessary to please God. When God sees a Christian's faith, He will not be ashamed to be called his God (Hebrews 11:6-16).

5. Faith is the only avenue to God and to the claiming of God's promises and blessings (Romans 4:5; 5:2; Hebrews 4:2).

6. Faith in God and His promises results in assurance, rest, and peace, not only in salvation but also in every detail of a Christian's life (II Peter 1:4; Hebrews 4:9-12; Philippians 4:6-7).

7. Faith, or walking in faith, is having complete trust and confidence in God and is not being dependent on feeling or intellectual understanding (II Corinthians 5:7; Proverbs 3:5-6).

8. Faith is tested in life's adverse situations, and the faith response of the Spirit-filled Christian is thanksgiving and praise (Habakkuk 3:17-19; Ephesians 5:20).

9. Faith, in a setting of prayer and fasting, becomes a powerful means of producing miraculous results (Matthew 17:14-21).

10. The measure of faith is the extent of one's willingness to crucify self daily and to live a life of obedience dedicated to serving God (Galatians 2:20; Romans 12:1; Luke 9:23).

The ten principles above are amply illustrated in the lives of the saints in the Old and New Testaments. Chapter 11 of Hebrews lists many of the heroes of faith in God's Hall of Fame. They portrayed faithfulness, which is faith lived out through their lives, even unto death. Remembering personal faith victories and blessings from one's life and the lives of others as illustrations of the above principles brings a reality to the Spirit-filled faith walk. Faith was the focal point of the revival in the church during the Reformation, and so it will be in the Christian's life. "The just shall live by faith" (Galatians 3:11).

**How you live and react in difficult and impossible situations indicates the strength of your faith in God (Hebrews 11:33-34).**

*A Belief in God's Promises*

The Christian faith of a Spirit-filled believer is based on the promises of God and, therefore, it is important for every born-again Christian to know, believe, memorize, and apply significant promises from the Word of God. The promises need to be applied in every situation of decision making and goal setting and in adverse circumstances and trials. General promises can become life-guiding principles that are foundations of Christian character. Significant general promises to be memorized are as follows:

- Salvation: John 1:12-13; 3:16, 36; I John 5:11-13
- Eternal assurance: John 10:28-29; Romans 8:38-39; I Peter 1:5
- Death: Psalm 23:4; II Corinthians 5:1, 6-8
- Rapture: I Thessalonians 4:16-17; Titus 2:13
- Heaven: John 14:1-3; I Peter 1:3-4; Revelation 21:1-4; 22:1-5

- Scripture: Psalm 119:9, 11, 15, 17, 89, 165; II Timothy 3:15-17; II Peter 1:3
- Prayer: II Chronicles 7:14; John 16:24
- Obedience: John 14:21; I Corinthians 10:13
- Mind: II Timothy 1:7; II Corinthians 10:5; Philippians 2:5-11; 4:7
- Giving: Proverbs 3:9-10; Luke 6:38; II Corinthians 9:6-8
- Soulwinning: Psalm 126:5-6; II Corinthians 5:11, 14, 15, 19, 20
- Peace: Isaiah 26:3; Philippians 4:7
- Power: Ephesians 3:20; Philippians 4:13
- Need: Philippians 4:19; Romans 8:32
- Training children: Proverbs 22:6; Ephesians 6:1-4

There are promises for every situation and circumstance of life. It is up to us to claim and apply them, and thereby our faith is strengthened and we take on more of Christ's likeness.

**How you live and apply God's promises is a testimony of your faith in God and His Word.**

### Walking in God's Faith-Rest

For every believer there is faith-rest that is temporal as well as eternal, mentioned in Hebrews 4:1-16. This is the rest from worry and anxiety about past, present, and future events and situations. This rest is available by believing and trusting in the promises of God (vv. 9-16). The Jews did not enter into the temporal rest God had promised because they did not have faith in the promises of God of which they were all aware (v. 2). When we do not have faith in the promises of God, we cannot experience the rest and peace of soul and mind that is available to us.

### Walking in God's Grace by Faith

Grace is God's unmerited favor and mercy upon the ill-deserved and is available to us not only in our salvation but also in God's provision for us in our Spirit-led walk in faith. Our faith in Jesus Christ's atonement and His promises of eternal life brought us salvation and was the start of our faith walk in the Spirit. Our faith in Christ and His promises should continue in every circumstance throughout our Christian life. We have faith in Christ and His Word, and He responds with His grace. God's grace is not bestowed on us because of our works but as the result of our faith in His promises found in His Word. God promised that His grace is sufficient to meet all of our needs (II Corinthians 12:9). Therefore, we have nothing of which to boast (Ephesians 2:8-9). The indwelling of the Spirit, filling of the Spirit, and walking in the Spirit are solely by God's grace and accessed only by faith (Romans 5:1-2).

### *Passing on a Heritage of Faith*

A heritage is something that is possessed by one person and passed on to someone else who follows after. To the unsaved, heritage is often nothing more than material possessions, which are passed to family and survivors through wills, trusts, and gifts.

For the family of God, however, the important thing that must be passed on is a spiritual heritage of faith–the gospel and the principles and promises from the Word of God–which is extended to others through teaching, preaching, example, and prayer. The gospel and the Bible life principles enable men not only to obtain eternal life but also to live lives that glorify and please the Lord.

Today, a battle is raging over which heritage will be passed on. Many young people are receiving a corrupt heritage from public schools, their peers, and the media. The Devil will make sure that this bad seed that has been sown sprouts into reeds blowing in the wind of humanistic thinking, brambles of sensual behavior, and weeds of materialistic desires.

Mature, Spirit-filled Christians, however, can have a powerful influence on those who follow after if they seize every opportunity to plant and water the seeds of the gospel and Bible principles and promises in the fertile soil of the minds and hearts of the young people they contact. As this godly heritage is sown, God is responsible for the harvest of mighty trees of righteousness and character, sweet fruits of truth and virtue, and fragrant flowers of love and grace (Isaiah 61:3).

In II Timothy 1:3, Paul mentions the heritage he received from his forefathers. In verse 5 he then refers to the heritage that Timothy received from his grandmother Lois and his mother, Eunice. In chapter 2 he admonishes Timothy to pass on the heritage that he has received. In Psalm 16:6, the writer declares that he has a goodly heritage. In Psalm 78 and 145 the psalmist urges the people not to hide their spiritual heritage but to show it to the coming generations, emphasizing the praises of the Lord, His strength, and His wonderful works. Teachers and parents should reiterate to those in their care God's majesty, power, past performance, and present miracles, especially as they have been manifested in their own lives with the Holy Spirit in control.

Salvation sets a person's desire to live a life that pleases and glorifies the Lord. Bible principles, promises, and faith are the means to accomplish that desire. The Spirit-filled walk of faith enables born-again Christians to have a life of victory over the world, sin, and death. "For whatsoever is born of God overcometh the world: and this is the victory that overcometh the world, even our faith. Who is he that overcometh the world, but he that believeth that Jesus is the Son of God?" (I John 5:4-5; Romans 8:37-39).

Walking in the Spirit can be summed up with a description of a spiritual person. A Spirit-filled, joyful Christian walking in the Spirit by faith has the following characteristics:

1. He reflects the character of Christ by exhibiting the nine qualities of spiritual character given in Galatians 5:22-23. He has constant communion with God through prayer and meditation on His Word.

2. He daily confesses his sin and walks in the light of God's forgiveness and cleansing. He would rather be holy by obedience to Christ's commands and will than be happy with the carnal lusts of the flesh and the world.

3. He has a spirit of thanksgiving, praise, and joy in the Lord even in the face of suffering, afflictions, and persecution. His positive faith attitude stems from a trust in God's promises.

4. He has an attitude of humble, sacrificial servanthood. He would rather serve than be served and rejoices when others succeed and prosper.

5. He has compassion for people that indicates the love for Christ in his heart. He reaches out to the unsaved with the gospel and to the saved with edification and encouragement.

6. He has an eternal perspective rather than being time oriented. He is looking forward to the rapture (blessed hope) and death holds no terror for him.

7. He is a student of the Word of God in which Jesus Christ's will is revealed, and as a result is able to discern matters and make decisions from God's viewpoint. He is receptive to the voice of God, not only through the Scriptures and his conscience but also through God's glorious works of Creation. He is aware that the Holy Spirit speaks in rejoicing, in sorrow, in his contemplation about God, and in daily provisions and miracles that are usually taken for granted. "The words that I speak unto you, they are spirit, and they are life" (John 6:63).

Do the above characteristics depict your Christian life?

True spirituality and a Spirit-filled walk are a continual reliance and dependence on Christ and on the power of the Holy Spirit to progressively imprint the likeness of Christ in our daily life. Paul in his letter to the Ephesians capsuled his purpose and desire for their spiritual walk. "For this cause I bow my knees unto the Father of our Lord Jesus Christ, of whom the whole family in heaven and earth is named, that he would grant you, according to the riches of his glory, to be strengthened with might by his Spirit in the inner man; that Christ may dwell in your hearts by faith; that ye, being rooted and grounded in love, may be able to comprehend with all saints what is the breadth, and length, and depth, and height; and to know the love of Christ, which passeth knowledge, that ye might be filled with all the fullness of God. Now unto him that is able to do exceeding abundantly above all that we ask or think, according to the power that worketh in us, unto him be glory in the church by Christ Jesus throughout all ages, world without end. Amen" (Ephesians 3:14-21).

Chapter 8

# GIFTS OF THE HOLY SPIRIT FOR BELIEVERS TODAY

The Holy Spirit gives gifts to the people of God today that are just as important and vital for the work of God as they were in the early church. Some of these gifts are special educational gifts, which are limited to the leaders in the body of believers. Many other gifts are encouraging gifts and are primarily ones that the Holy Spirit has imparted to all believers. Some gifts, called enhancing (sign) gifts, are inactive now because they were given only to enhance and authenticate the apostles' proclamation of the gospel until the church was firmly established and the Word of God was completed circa A.D. 95-125. The main teaching on spiritual gifts is found in Romans 12:3-8; I Corinthians 12; Ephesians 4:1-16; and I Peter 4:8-11.

The emphasis of this teaching is that all Christians at salvation are baptized into the body of Christ and, in spite of their diversities, are to be one in that body. They come into that body with different personalities, backgrounds, positions in life, ideas, desires, and ways of doing things. They also attain different levels of growth in their Christian lives. Therefore, God equips all believers with one or more special gifts in such ways that, whatever their backgrounds and differences might be, all believers are needed and will fit into the body of believers. These gifts uniquely qualify them to be a part of the local assembly of believers and to make a vital contribution.

When these believers have dedicated their lives to the Lord and are walking spiritually in their relationship with the Lord and with others, the use of their gifts in the body of believers will help bring unity to the body and meet the needs of the body as well.

### *Definition of the Gifts of the Holy Spirit*

A spiritual gift is a supernatural ability given by the grace of God at salvation to every believer to serve one another for the common good of the body of Christ and to bring glory to God (I Peter 4:10; I Corinthians 12:7, 11; 14:4). The believer is empowered to use his gift when he is initially filled with the Holy Spirit at dedication. Gifts are not the same as the fruit of the Spirit (Galatians 5:22-23). Fruit is a singular noun describing character qualities that are the result of a Spirit-filled life.

God, in His unlimited creativeness and foreknowledge, gives individuals at conception one or more talents and superintends the development of those talents through training and experience into distinctive abilities (James 1:17). God usually uses natural talents or provides the needed abilities when He bestows the supernatural gifts; therefore, there is a wide diversity of each person's gifts although the gifts may have the same label. Just as individuals' fingerprints are not alike, so individual gifts of the Holy Spirit are not alike. The individual gifts vary in where and how they are used. For example, the gift of teaching can be used in the pulpit, in the Christian classroom or Bible study, in the home, in counseling, in the writing of Christian materials and books, and so forth.

### Three Categories of Gifts

There are certain supernatural gifts listed in the Word of God, but theologians differ about the number depending on their definitions of spiritual gifts. Since there are five different lists given in the Word of God and no two are exactly alike, it is probable that these are not a complete listing of all gifts. More than likely, the lists contain only the gifts that were to be emphasized in those particular passages. The following is one way of grouping supernatural gifts under three categories. The first two are given in I Peter 4:10-11 as ministry, or educating, and service, or encouraging, gifts. The last category is given in Hebrews 2:3-4 as sign gifts.

1. Educating gifts given to Christians who are the leaders in the body of Christ.
2. Encouraging gifts imparted to all believers for service to others.
3. Enhancing (sign) gifts bestowed on first-century Christians to validate the proclamation of the gospel. These are now inactive gifts because they are no longer necessary or useful to the body of Christ.

### The Educating Gifts

First, God gives special educating (ministry) gifts to leaders in the church. These are to be used to reach unbelievers and for the nurturing of and ministering to the body of believers. Special qualifications are required and special titles and responsibilities are given to those chosen by God for these purposes. The main passage that identifies and explains the educating gifts is found in Ephesians 4:11-15.

> And he gave some, apostles; and some, prophets; and some, evangelists; and some, pastors and teachers; for the perfecting of the saints, for the work of the ministry, for the edifying of the body of Christ: till we all come in the unity of the

### Table 7
### Gifts of the Holy Spirit

| | Rom. 12:6-8 | I Cor. 12:8-10 | I Cor. 12:28-30 | Eph. 4:11-12 | I Pet. 4:10-11 |
|---|---|---|---|---|---|
| **Active Gifts** | | | | | |
| **Educating (Ministry)** | | | | I Pet. 4:10-11 | |
| 1. Evangelist | | | | 4:11 | |
| 2. Pastor | | | | 4:11 | |
| 3. Teacher | 12:7 | | 12:28 | 4:11 | |
| **Encouraging (Serving)** | | | | I Pet. 4:10-11 | |
| 4. Words of Wisdom | | 12:8 | | | |
| 5. Faith | | 12:9 | | | |
| 6. Distinguishing of Spirits | | 12:10 | | | |
| 7. Administration | 12:8 | | 12:28 | | |
| 8. Serving | 12:7 | | 12:28 | | 4:11 |
| 9. Exhortation | 12:8 | | | 4:12 | |
| 10. Giving | 12:8 | | | | |
| 11. Mercy | 12:8 | | | | |
| **Inactive Gifts** | | | | | |
| **Enhancing (Sign)** | | | | Hebrews 2:3-4 | |
| 1. Apostleship | | | 12:28 | 4:11 | |
| 2. Prophecy | 12:6 | 12:10 | 12:28 | 4:11 | |
| 3. Knowledge | | 12:8 | 12:28 | | |
| 4. Miracles | | 12:10 | 12:28 | | |
| 5. Healing | | 12:9 | 12:28 | | |
| 6. Tongues and Interpretation | | 12:10 | | | |

faith, and of the knowledge of the Son of God, unto a perfect man, unto the measure of the stature of the fulness of Christ: that we henceforth be no more children, tossed to and fro, and carried about with every wind of doctrine, by the sleight of men, and cunning craftiness, whereby they lie in wait to deceive; but speaking the truth in love, may grow up into him in all things, which is the head, even Christ.

Among these five leaders in the church of that day, the apostles and prophets are no longer needed or present in the church. The other leaders named in this list—evangelists, pastors, and teachers—are still present in the church today and have a necessary and vital place in the ministry of the church.

- Evangelizing (Ephesians 4:11). This is the ability to proclaim and explain the gospel message with unusual clarity. The evangelist often travels to many different areas and churches. The gift, however, may be used in many different soulwinning endeavors.
- Pastoring (Ephesians 4:11). This is the ability to spiritually shepherd, provide for, care for, and protect a group of believers.
- Teaching (Romans 12:7; I Corinthians 12:28; Ephesians 4:11). This is the ability to explain God's truths to God's people. Most pastors and some evangelists have this gift.

As their titles suggest, these men are directly responsible under the control and guidance of the Holy Spirit for sharing the Word of God with the body of believers and the lost, for planting churches, and also for giving spiritual direction and nurture to the church. They are not only fitted but also called to the ministry by the direct intervention of God in their lives.

"Ye have not chosen me, but I have chosen you, and ordained you, that ye should go and bring forth fruit, and that your fruit should remain" (John 15:16).

Those with the gifts of ministry are called and equipped by God to train the members of the church for the work of God. God has set standards designed to assure that the wrong men will not be chosen or that the position will not be misused (I Timothy 3:1-7; Titus 1:7-9). If those who minister displease God in their personal lives or in the way they conduct themselves, God can judge and remove them at any time. Moses experienced such judgment (Numbers 20:12), and Paul later was aware that this could happen to his own ministry (I Corinthians 9:27).

*The Encouraging Gifts*

All Christians have one or more of these gifts to be used to encourage and serve fellow believers and to make gospel contacts with unbelievers.

- Word of wisdom (I Corinthians 12:8). This is the ability to understand, interpret, communicate, and apply Bible doctrines, principles, and promises to life. Pastors, Bible teachers, and evangelists usually have this gift, but many laymen have the same gift.
- Faith (I Corinthians 12:9). This is the ability to trust God and His promises for great and mighty works and to supply needs.
- Distinguishing the spirits (I Corinthians 12:10). This is the ability to judge character and determine whether a person is motivated by the Holy Spirit or by the world, the flesh, and the Devil. This gift is used, especially by Christian laymen, to determine whether evangelists, pastors, or teachers are proclaiming the Word of God.
- Leadership, or administration (Romans 12:8; I Corinthians 12:28). Leadership is the ability to motivate or influence others to want to accomplish the same God-glorifying goals that the leader has for the group. Administration is

the ability to apply the functions of leadership, which are planning, deciding, delegating, organizing, and supervising.

- Service, or helps (Romans 12:7; I Corinthians 12:28; Ephesians 4:12; I Peter 4:11). This the ability to be of assistance to those who have a need.
- Exhortation (Romans 12:8). This is the ability to correct, admonish, comfort, and encourage believers and nonbelievers.
- Giving (Romans 12:8). This is the ability to be generous with time, energy, money, and things with which God has blessed, without any expectation of return or profit.
- Mercy (Romans 12:8). This is the ability to show compassion and give help to the weak, sick, and disabled. It also involves forgiving and loving enemies without a desire for retaliation or vengeance.

All gifts must be exercised in the spirit of love, or they will be unprofitable (I Corinthians 13:1-7). Charles Ryrie in *Basic Theology* (p. 428) noted that God has given commands to all believers to minister in the many areas of spiritual gifts. The list below has been adapted from his list. All believers are commanded to function in nine of the eleven areas of active gifts whether or not they have a special gift.

Our very relationship with the Lord and the presence of the Lord in our lives by the Holy Spirit require that we all use our gifts, at least in measure, in all kinds of spiritual ministry to others in the body of Christ. This is part of the character of true Christians. Some believers are especially gifted in certain areas of the Christian life and are called to make contributions to the body of believers as they devote their lives to the exercise of these gifts.

Satan is a clever enemy who is constantly working against the purposes of God and the people of God. He can easily arouse in leaders and ordinary believers a fleshly spirit of pride and arrogance

*Table 8*

**Spiritual Gifts**

| Spiritual Gifts | Commands Given to All Believers |
|---|---|
| 1. Evangelizing | 1. Great Commission (Matthew 28:19) |
| 2. Teaching | 2. Teach and admonish (Colossians 3:16) |
| 3. Expressing wisdom | 3. Ask for wisdom (James 1:5) |
| 4. Having faith | 4. Walk by faith (II Corinthians 5:7) |
| 5. Distinguishing spirits | 5. Try the spirits (I John 4:1) |
| 6. Serving/helping | 6. Serve one another (Galatians 5:13) |
| 7. Exhorting | 7. Exhort one another (Hebrews 10:25) |
| 8. Giving | 8. Give cheerfully (II Corinthians 9:6-8) |
| 9. Showing mercy | 9. Be kind and tenderhearted (Ephesians 4:32) |
| 10. Pastoring | 10. ———————— |
| 11. Leading/administering | 11. ———————— |

because of the gifts God has given them. Rather than using these gifts for the glory of God and the service of the body of believers, these people yield to Satan's promptings to build up themselves, enhance their own reputations, and fulfill their own desires.

In truly Spirit-filled and Spirit-controlled believers, God receives all the glory and praise in the giving and the use of these gifts, and no one but Christ.

*Suggestions for New Believers*

1. Dedicate your life to the Lord, giving Him complete control so that you can be daily filled (controlled) with the Spirit.

2. Use your natural talents and develop your abilities and skills in a fundamental Bible-believing church when opportunities become available.

3. Ask God to reveal your gift and trust Him to do so in His time, as you are active in the Lord's work. It will be something you desire and enjoy doing in your ministry of serving others. It will also be an area in which the Lord opens opportunities of service.

4. Do not neglect, but stir up or rekindle, the gift(s) that have been given to you (I Timothy 4:14; II Timothy 1:6). This can be done by setting eternal priorities (Matthew 6:33; Colossians 3:2) and, also, by getting additional education and experience.

5. Be willing to use the gift(s) for full-time ministry to the glory of God.

6. Be sensitive to the guidance of the Holy Spirit and His leading by the Word of God.

Being busy in the Lord's work, serving others, is the best way to discover your gift(s). Once you discover your gift(s), make sure you use it for the glory of the Lord.

The inactive enhancing (sign) gifts will be discussed in chapter 9.

Chapter 9

# THE ENHANCING "SIGN" GIFTS, WHICH ARE NOW INACTIVE

There is an emphasis that has not been known since about A.D. 150 and was only revived early in this century. It has to do with the belief that the "sign" gifts of the New Testament are necessary for believers today and must be taught and practiced in local churches.

Because of the danger that the present emphasis may not be scriptural and may actually detract from other ministries of the Holy Spirit, it is important to examine today's teachings in the light of the Scriptures to see what the Scriptures actually teach about them.

The enhancing gifts, including the sign gifts, which are now inactive, are as follows:

*Apostles*

The gift of the apostles was the ability to proclaim the teachings of Jesus, including the gospel and the establishing of churches, and was accompanied by signs, miracles, and wonders unique to the church of that day. The office ceased when the last of the apostles, John, died sometime after A.D. 95. The requirement for apostleship was that the man had been with Jesus and had received His teachings. We know that the twelve disciples were apostles and that Matthias replaced Judas after he committed suicide. There may have been more apostles, such as the seventy whom Jesus sent on a preaching tour or the one hundred twenty gathered in the Upper Room. These men were the first preachers of the gospel, called, trained, and equipped by the Lord Himself to lead the initial task of carrying the gospel. Paul was later added to their number as the apostle to the Gentiles (Galatians 1:12; 2:7).

The apostles were not only given the power to do miracles but also gifted with special authority from the Lord to minister, rule, and advise in the churches in ways leaders today cannot. Such strong authority was necessary in that day when the gospel was first being preached and the church was in its infancy. Some of the apostles, including Paul, Peter, and John, were also used to write New Testament books under the divine inspiration of the Holy Spirit. They, therefore, had a unique function in the church, and when that function ended, the gift of apostles also ended.

### Prophets

The gift of the prophets was the ability to receive special revelations from God to the church in the absence of a written New Testament. The requirement and test for God's prophets were that they be accurate 100 percent of the time in their prophecies (Deuteronomy 18:20-22). There were others who had the gift of prophecy besides the apostles, e.g., Philip's four unmarried daughters (Acts 21:9). The church needed the exhortation, edification, and comfort that these prophets received from God since the complete Word of God was not yet available (I Corinthians 14:3-4). The prophets are mentioned in I Corinthians 12 and 14 but are also referred to in Acts. Since God's revelation of scriptural truth was completed by A.D. 95, this gift also passed away shortly after that time.

## Knowledge

The gift of knowledge was the ability to receive from God new revelations and to proclaim them to the other believers. It had to do mainly with the encouragement and edification of the believers in the church by showing that God was still revealing His truth to His people. This is emphasized many times in I Corinthians 14. Some of these revelations had to do with the present events that needed to be understood, such as the famine of Acts 11:28-30, Paul's imprisonment in Acts 21:10-14, and other future events.

Prophecy and knowledge are, of necessity, very closely related. Prophecy would have to do with revelations themselves and knowledge would be the ability to understand and apply the revelations.

First Corinthians 13:8-10 indicates that prophecy, knowledge, and tongues—which represent the sign gifts—will cease, while faith, hope, and love will continue during the church age. In verse 10 the phrase "that which is perfect is come" refers to the completion of the New Testament. As Paul explained in verse 9, until that time everything was a partial revelation and there was a need for prophecy and knowledge. The complete, or perfect, Word of God is now sufficient for "all things that pertain unto life and godliness" (II Peter 1:3). It is also "profitable for doctrine, for reproof, for correction, for instruction in righteousness" (II Timothy 3:16).

In the churches, tongues were spoken and interpreted by the apostles and believers who had the special gift. As in the Corinthian church (I Corinthians 14), the church members were not to forbid the use of tongues as long as God's commands concerning the use of tongues were followed (I Corinthians 14:25-39). With the completion of the New Testament and the foundational establishment of the fledging church, there was no need for the apostles, with their supernatural knowledge authenticated by miracles, signs, and wonders, or the prophets with their totally accurate predictions and explanations of the present and future events.

*The Sign Gifts*

These gifts included the ability to perform miracles such as raising the dead, casting out demons, healing instantaneously, and speaking in tongues, as well as other signs and wonders performed during the formation of the early church before the completion of the written Word of God. By the end of the first century the enhancing (sign) gifts were no longer needed and became inactive. However, the Holy Spirit still works today in unusual and miraculous ways within the guidelines given in the Word of God. "Never the Spirit without the Word and never the Word without the Spirit" was the principle used during the Reformation.

**Miracles** was the ability to perform instantaneous, supernatural acts. The Book of Acts indicates that this gift was one given mainly to the apostles, including Paul, and was used by them to aid in the first preaching of the gospel to the unsaved. With this gift, the disciples were given the power to bring about healings as proof that the blessing and approval of God were upon them and that what they were proclaiming was truly a message from God that all were to believe. Second Corinthians 12:12, in fact, identifies these as "signs of the apostles." This also seems to be the intention of Jesus in His teaching in Mark 16:17-18. Hebrews 2:3-4 bears this out:

> How shall we escape, if we neglect so great salvation; which at the first began to be spoken by the Lord, and was confirmed unto us by them that heard him; God also bearing them witness, both with signs and wonders, and with divers miracles, and gifts of the Holy Ghost, according to his own will?

Miracles were often used in Acts but are seldom mentioned in the epistles. Two of the times when miracles were not used are the curing of Paul's own illness in II Corinthians 12:7-10 or that of Epaphroditus in Philippians 2:25-30.

**Healing** was the ability to bring about miraculous, instantaneous cure for a disease or a physical or mental disability. The Scriptures teach that God is still able to heal today but that He does not give this power of healing to men. It can come only through prayer and according to His will. Many times God will, in fact, choose not to bring healing. Today God performs miraculous healing as follows (James 5:14-16). If any are sick they should follow these steps: Call for the elders of the church. Confess all sins. Have the elders anoint with oil and pray. The prayers of righteous men in faith will see miraculous healing, if it is God's will. Often God uses medical means to heal, but God does the healing.

**Tongues** was the ability given to New Testament believers to speak in languages other than their own language without any previous study or knowledge of those other languages.

The purpose of this gift was mainly to aid in the witness of the gospel to the unsaved by giving proof for the divine origin of the gospel and showing that Jesus was truly being proclaimed as the promised Messiah and Savior. This is clearly taught both in Acts and in I Corinthians 14. In Acts, on the only three occasions when tongues were used, three different types of people responded to the gospel: the Jews in Acts 2, the Gentiles in Acts 10, and the followers of John the Baptist in Acts 19. This agrees with I Corinthians 14:22, which states that "tongues are a sign to them that believe not." Tongues, as used in I Corinthians 14, refers to the same gift of tongues given at Pentecost (Acts 2:4). It was an unknown tongue, or language, to some people, but it was a known language to other individuals from a foreign country. Nowhere does Scripture say that it was some "heavenly" language, nor can it be related to the groaning of the Holy Spirit as we pray (Romans 8:26). Mysterious verbal utterance or babblings were a part of Greek pagan religious ritual and still exist today in many pagan religions, e.g., voodoo ceremonies of Haiti and Africa and some pagan rites in India and the Far East. Corinth was a port city on the seagoing trade route between the Near East and Italy and ports beyond. During the winter, ships would be anchored there for some time awaiting favorable sailing weather. If the foreigners were to hear the gospel, there had to be the gift of tongues and their interpretation. Paul placed a high value on the ability of the gift of tongues because it was so useful in spreading the gospel (I Corinthians 14:5), but he did not mean that all Christians were to speak in tongues. Paul preached to many cultures with different languages, hence, his statement that he spoke "with tongues more than ye all" (I Corinthians 14:18-19). We have preached in foreign countries, and we would not preach or teach in a foreign assembly without an interpreter because we do not have the gift of tongues. The gift of tongues would be very useful today for missionaries who have to spend a great deal of time studying the language before they can communicate the gospel, but God has not chosen to renew this gift.

*Pentecostalism*

The Pentecostals sprang out of the Holiness movement of the nineteenth century and are responsible for the renewed interest in the Holy Spirit and the promotion of the sign gifts, especially the gifts of healing and tongues. They use spirited experience-centered worship as a vehicle for promotion of their denominational teaching.

Though spirited worship occurred before the end of the nineteenth century, Pentecostalism has its roots in a Holiness gathering at Bethel Bible College in 1901 in Topeka, Kansas, and is based in Methodist Charles F. Parham's interpretation of Acts 2:4 that speaking in tongues was the initial evidence of the "baptism of the Holy Spirit." Miraculous healings by laying on of hands were also part of the beliefs. There were many female preachers and pastors in the early years of the Pentecostal movement. The best-known Pentecostal woman of the twentieth century was evangelist Aimee Semple McPherson, founder of the International Church of the Foursquare Gospel. Pentecostal theology is based in Wesleyan Holiness doctrine, which teaches entire sanctification (sinless perfection or purity of motive), baptism of the Holy Spirit apart from salvation (second work of grace), speaking in tongues, and loss of salvation by deliberately sinning. The Pentecostal exuberant mode of worship has its roots in African religious rituals rather than the historical development of European church worship since the Reformation.

The Keswick (deeper life) movement of the 1870s was also a Holiness influence on Pentecostalism. The Keswick doctrine displaced the Wesleyan concept of eradication and replaced it with an endowment of power. A. B. Simpson, founder of the Christian Missionary Alliance denomination, emphasized the Keswick brand of sanctification and the dispensational teaching of premillennialism. He rejected the teaching that the baptism of the Holy Spirit was always accompanied by speaking in tongues but did not discourage or forbid the speaking of tongues in Alliance churches.

In 1906 in Los Angeles, the three-year Azusa Street Revival, led by black pastor William J. Seymour, served as a catalyst to help spread the Pentecostal movement worldwide. Pentecostals were originally interracial until about 1925, when the social climate, particularly in the South and Midwest, forced division in many churches and associations. The Pentecostal Holiness Church was first to adopt a Pentecostal statement of faith in 1908. In 1914, the Assemblies of God was formed.

There are many different branches and variations of belief in Pentecostalism but all believe that sign gifts are active today. The old-time Methodists and the Church of the Nazarene teach entire sanctification but do not practice tongues. The Assemblies of God, the largest Pentecostal denomination, and the Foursquare Gospel churches believe in progressive sanctification but espouse tongues as the initial evidence of the "baptism" of the Spirit. The Church of God, the Church of God of Prophecy, and the Pentecostal Holiness Church teach not only entire santification but also tongues as the initial evidence of being Spirit filled.

Pentecostals believe we are now in the last days (the latter rain) when God will pour out His Spirit and manifest the sign gifts as mentioned in Acts 2:17-18 according to the prophecy of Joel 2:28-32. They reject the historic fundamentalist interpretation of I Corinthians 13:8-10 as being the time of the closing of the cannon and the cessation of the sign gifts about A.D. 150. They view this interpretation as being unlikely in the light of I Corinthians 13:12. Pentecostals also interpret I Corinthians 14:2-4 and 22 as being ecstatic spiritual utterances rather than foreign languages.

At the end of the twentieth century, Pentecostalism was one of the fastest-growing segments of the Christian world, particularly in Korea, Africa, and South America. There are eleven thousand Pentecostal or charismatic denominations in the world. It is growing at the rate of thirteen million people annually, or thirty-five thousand a day. With nearly a half billion adherents, it is the second largest Christian group after Roman Catholicism.

Historically, Pentecostal churches have attracted the poor or working class with limited education, who need concrete experiential evidence to buttress their faith and who prefer to be more emotionally expressive in their praise and worship. In the last half of the twentieth century, Pentecostalism was promoted among the middle class by *Christian Life* magazine; various

Pentecostal television stations, which now include satellite networks; and the popularity of ministries of Oral Roberts, Pat Robertson, Katherine Kuhlman, David Wilkerson, Guy du Plesses, Ernest Angley, Benny Hinn, Jimmy Swaggart, Bishop T. D. Jakes, and Bishop Charles Blake Sr. In recent decades many of the elements of Pentecostal worship, such as band music, clapping, and charismatic manifestations, especially of tongues and healing, have made inroads into mainline denominations and spawned the ecumenical, interdenominational charismatic movement, e.g., the Promise Keepers and the Full Gospel Businessmen's Fellowship International.

One of the most informative books on the history and development of the modern Pentecostal movement is *Aspects of Pentecostal Charismatic Origin*, edited by Vinson Gynan and published by Logos. It consists of the twelve lectures delivered by Pentecostal scholars at Lee College in Cleveland, Tennessee, in 1973 on five developmental phases of Pentecostalism in the U.S. The scholars represented the larger denominations of Pentecostalism. The editor, in 1975, reported this prediction about the movement: "Some experts have predicted that after another generation or so, the majority of all the Christians in the world will probably be nonwhite from the southern hemisphere and Pentecostal." At the start of the twenty-first century the prediction has almost been fulfilled.

The Pentecostals' attributes are their renewed emphasis on constantly being filled with the Holy Spirit and zeal for prayer, praise, witnessing, missions, and dependence on God. These are things with which we agree. However, Fundamentalist biblical Christianity questions not only their strange interpretations of Scripture that form their doctrinal distinctives but also their mode of worship, such as unrestrained emotionalism, use of contemporary rock music, promotion of the inactive sign gifts, and giving preeminence to the Holy Spirit instead of Jesus

Christ. Fundamentalist biblical Christians need to deal with Pentecostals with a spirit of love as Christian brothers. Pentecostals need teaching in Bible doctrine instead of ridicule, and direction rather than derision. In addition to debating the question of whether the sign gifts have ceased or not seeking some specific sign gift, we should be asking the question, "Am I using the gift that God has given to me to His glory?"

### Summary

The Holy Spirit always works within a biblical framework, but we must be careful not to expect the Holy Spirit to be contained in our little theological or denominational framework. There is also a fleshly tendency to expect the Holy Spirit to work within our agenda, prescribing for Him when, where, and how He should work.

Jesus compared the Holy Spirit to the wind. "The wind bloweth where it listeth, and thou hearest the sound thereof, but canst not tell whence it cometh, and whither it goeth: so is every one that is born of the Spirit" (John 3:8). We are taught a similar truth about the Holy Spirit's giving us our gifts in I Corinthians 12:11. "But all these worketh that one and the selfsame Spirit, dividing to every man severally as he will." We are just among the players in the game of life, and we are required to play by the rules in the Word of God. We cannot be the referee, the coach, or the owner of the team, but we must not be a mere spectator.

God, through the Holy Spirit, works when, where, and how He chooses but always according to the Word of God and always to glorify Christ and His plan of redemption. God never thwarts His purpose and plan for an individual, the church, or the world.

Chapter 10

# CONCLUSION

To live a joyful, Spirit-filled life and have power, guidance, and spiritual fruit in our lives, it is necessary to have knowledge of and contact with the Holy Spirit, the third person of the Trinity. This knowledge and contact must be based on the sure Word of God and not on a subjective emotional experience that some have had or imagine they should have. Our contact depends on two pivotal decisions. The first decision is the salvation decision as the result of the Holy Spirit's conviction. We turn from our sin and receive Christ as Savior and Lord. The Holy Spirit enters our lives, and we experience the peace and joy of our eternal salvation. The second decision is a dedication decision when we abandon our self-centered lives and turn the control of our lives completely over to the control (filling) of the Holy Spirit, making the Lord Jesus Christ preeminent in our lives. We start daily denying self and abiding in Christ, experiencing a renewed sense of Christ's presence, fullness of joy, and fervent love.

The result is a strong desire to bring our lifestyle into conformity to the image of Christ by letting the Holy Spirit purge our lives of sinful habits. Daily walking in the Spirit by faith in willing obedience to the commands of Christ assures us of the abundant life in Christ. The Holy Spirit strengthens our loving relationship with others by helping us to have a servant's heart, thus promoting unity in the church. He motivates and empowers us to serve the Lord using the gifts that God has given to proclaim the gospel, edify the saints, and do everything in love to His glory. We depend on God's grace, and the result is spiritual fruit in our lives and the lives of others.

God's grace offers to every Christian the exciting Spirit-filled life of service to God and others to be received by faith. Will you receive it by letting the Lord Jesus Christ have complete control and be the Lord of your life? The Holy Spirit gives the Spirit-filled believer the power and guidance to have daily victory over the flesh (self) to live a joyful life of love and humble service to God and others, producing spiritual fruit.

> These things have I spoken unto you, that my joy might remain in you, and that your joy might be full. This is my commandment, That ye love one another, as I have loved you (John 15:11-12).

> For the joy of the Lord is your strength (Nehemiah 8:10).

> Whom having not seen, ye love; in whom, though now ye see him not, yet believing, ye rejoice with joy unspeakable and full of glory: receiving the end of your faith, even the salvation of your souls (I Peter 1:8-9).

Appendix A

# THE HOLY SPIRIT IN THE LIFE
# OF A MISSIONARY AND A TEACHER

The Holy Spirit manifests Himself in the life of the Christian in many ways, but the following are the two most sought after in one's gospel ministry: (1) His leadership and guidance in everyday goals, plans, and decisions, both major and minor, (2) His power, especially his convicting power to change, to help, and to influence sinners and saints. The following is an account of the Holy Spirit at work in the life of two dedicated men—a missionary and a teacher.

### Background and Characteristics of the Authors—Carson and Walter Fremont

In their earlier years Carson and Walter grew up in Terre Haute, Indiana, with an older sister and a younger brother. Their father had a linotype business and their mother helped out in the business, so they had a live-in nanny to care for them. Father's business failed in the crash of 1929, and they moved to Fort Lauderdale, Florida, where Father took over as business manager of two newspapers. Two years later Father was in the hospital for three months as a result of an auto accident. They then moved to Wilmette, Illinois, where he took a job on the Evanston newspaper. In the heart of the depression that job lasted only a year. The family may have been poor, but they always had food and a nice, warm, modern home. Father had to be gone a good bit of one year, trying to find work in Ohio, and so Mother reared the four children that year.

The large Methodist church in Wilmette had a "Friendly Indians" organization, led by the assistant pastor of the church. Carson and Walter belonged to the group. Through that contact, their whole family attended the Sunday school and morning worship services of the church.

Mother had made a decision for Christ at the age of twelve and at that time became the pianist. Several years later she became the organist for the church she attended. Father made a decision for Christ in 1930 in Ft. Lauderdale. Mother always made sure the children regularly attended Sunday school and church. When the family moved to Dayton, Ohio, they attended a very liberal denominational church of the Disciples of Christ that Mother preferred. Father held the position of elder in that church for thirty years. A second sister was born in Dayton.

Mother, having been a schoolteacher, kept strict discipline over the children in an atmosphere of love. She was zealous in moral value training to the extent of tearing out all magazine advertisements about liquor and tobacco. She also forbade movies, which she called mind polluters. Father was stern and showed his love by telling exciting bedtime stories, and on weekends, teaching the boys to shoot his 22 rifle, taking them hiking, and practicing ball with them. On his two-week vacations, he took Carson, Walter, and their younger brother, Bill, tent camping and fishing on the Still Water River north of West Milton, Ohio, at the Spitler farm. The boys learned how to swim, row a boat, run a trotline, and eat fish two meals a day. When the boys were in junior high, Father took them to Lynch's fish camp on Sauble Lake north of Baldwin, Michigan. There they enjoyed the luxury of a log cabin, explored, swam, fished the chain of three lakes, and absorbed the sights, sounds, and smells of God's creation at its best. This included seeing beavers at work, a variety of birds, bears, and deer.

Father schooled the boys in the work ethic and frugality by requiring them to have a part-time job or newspaper route and to save 20 percent of all the money they earned.

Carson and Walter were very close and always shared a room with bunk beds. Carson was nineteen months younger than Walter and followed him everywhere during childhood. Both had musical abilities and played in the high school band and orchestra. Both had athletic abilities in swimming, baseball, basketball, and tennis. They learned to be highly disciplined in their Christian lives in morality, health habits, frugality, and spiritual matters. Carson tended to be shy but energetic and was an independent thinker with his own opinions. Walter was more gregarious, more vocal with his strong opinions. His dynamic creative energy sometimes led to trouble until he learned how to properly control it by planning and setting goals.

*The Work of the Holy Spirit in the Life of a Missionary: Carson*
*Kester Fremont (March 8, 1926)*

Some of my earliest childhood memories have to do with the first years of the depression, from 1931 to 1933, when Dad had lost his job and we were living north of Chicago. I cannot remember a single instance when anyone ever approached me about my need of a Savior or taught me anything about salvation. In Dayton, when I was ten, I was baptized by immersion, given a Bible, told to be a good boy and attend church all the time, and taken into the membership of the liberal Disciples of Christ church. I had no real conviction of sin or of a need for a Savior and thought I was all right.

When I was fourteen years old, my brother and I began to attend a Bible study club taught by a godly missionary who was home from China during the years of World War II. The teaching was altogether new to me. After a few weeks, in the late evening of December 31, 1940, we attended a watch night service in this missionary's home. He gave the gospel, and near the midnight hour, an invitation. Bob Brown, the same one who later reached my brother, purposely sat beside me and gave me a "holy poke" in the ribs. For the first time, the Holy Spirit showed me that I was a sinner and needed a Savior, and I was moved to respond with faith in Christ. We spent the next day in Xenia, Ohio, in the home of the businessman, Mr. Eavey, who had helped found this Bible study club, and I more fully realized what this decision had really meant.

From that time on, the Bible study club became a major part of my life, and I began to grow under this missionary's teaching from Romans. In the summer of 1941 I attended a youth conference at a campground on an island south of Miamisburg. At that conference I received the full assurance of my eternal salvation, determined to daily walk in obedience with the Lord in His Word, and realized the importance of prayer and witnessing.

The second summer after I was saved, my brother and I again attended the Bible club youth conference. On the Wednesday night of the conference, July 2, 1942, as I listened to a message from Romans 12:1-2, the Holy Spirit spoke to me about completely dedicating my life to the Lord, and at the same time, I felt the call to His service. I remember walking down the aisle that night, at the same time my brother did, to make this very firm decision.

At the time, because I was extremely shy and immature and still a very young Christian, no one would have advised me that I belonged in the ministry or on the mission field. However, I had the assurance from the Lord, by the Holy Spirit in my life, that He would take care of that in His good time and that I should trust Him in the matter.

I began to go out on street meetings with a group from a church near the one we attended. My brother and I began attending a church in our neighborhood, where we sat under the ministry of a godly Sunday school teacher. A number of other Christians in that church also had an influence on me. My brother and I soon learned to look to the Holy Spirit for guidance in the many decisions and situations we were to face. The following steps are the ones we generally follow to make sure the Holy Spirit is leading.

1. Ask the Lord to guide as soon as you sense the Holy Spirit is giving a strong desire to do a particular thing or make a specific decision.
2. Pray about it in the intervening time, trusting God to direct every step.
3. Go to God's Word to make sure the decision is in line with scriptural principles.
4. Talk it over with a godly friend or, if married, with your wife, since she is part of the team.
5. Wait on the Lord until He opens the door to the right circumstances and timing.
6. Give the Lord the praise and thanksgiving for the results that bring glory to His name.

In 1944, immediately after graduating from high school, I was taken into the army and sent to a field artillery base in Fayetteville, North Carolina. The Lord helped me to take a stand for Him in the barracks, and my personal walk with the Lord also grew. I also found other Christians in nearby units, and we began to go into Fayetteville on Saturday nights to hold street meetings at the town square. This was a test for me, for some of the fellows from our army unit would sometimes come and mock us as we sang and spoke. A Christian family in that city took us into their home on weekends.

In mid-1945, while the war with Japan was still being fought in the Philippines, I was part of a unit sent there. We saw little action. The war ended quickly after that, and we were sent back to Manila, where I spent my weekends participating in G. I. Gospel Hour meetings held in a large funeral parlor auditorium on a main street of the city. My main work was to deal with soldiers wanting to trust Christ. On some Saturday nights, we would get a jeep and hold meetings outside the city. Hal Webb, an evangelist, was one of my companions in those meetings. We also had a radio ministry.

After doing a lot of preaching and other types of work in some of the Filipino churches of the area, I was finally sent back on a large troopship to the United States to be discharged. As we were leaving Manila harbor on the ship, the Holy Spirit touched my heart, and I felt led to dedicate my life to being a foreign missionary. Though it was to be another seven years before I would return to the Philippines, the Lord never let me turn back from that decision.

In the years I was in Wheaton College and graduate school, the Lord led me to dedicate each of my summers to getting experience in camp work, pastoring, soulwinning, and other types of service for Him. One summer, a group of us from the college were chosen to travel all summer in meetings. I was the speaker for the group. Another summer, I pastored a small church south of Peoria, Illinois. The Holy Spirit brought a revival in that community. Among others, there were twenty-one young people who trusted the Lord through that ministry. The last two years before leaving for the mission field, I pastored a church near Chicago. As young as I was, the Holy Spirit was teaching me complete need for dependence upon His working in and through me and in the hearts of men and women.

At the college I attended, I held various offices, including chairman for all the groups who went into Chicago on Saturday nights and Sunday mornings for street meetings and soulwinning in the "bowery" section of Madison and State Streets. My companions in that work were mostly former soldiers who were also dedicated to serving the Lord. Among them was Jim Elliot, a close friend, who was killed in 1956 on a beach in Central America with four others. The Holy Spirit used these experiences to prepare us young men for further service for the Lord.

On February 10th, 1953, I was accepted as a missionary under the Association of Baptists for World Evangelism for service in the Philippines and went out to the field that very summer. I was single at the time and, after language study, was assigned to teach in a large seminary run by our mission in Manila. With that, during the vacation seasons, I also began to do youth conference work in various parts of the islands. That gave opportunity for much preaching and soulwinning. The last year of that five-year term, I was appointed the acting director of the school, a responsibility I continued to have for three more years after returning from furlough.

In early 1958 I came home on my first furlough. Darlene had come from Illinois and had been led to my home church as church secretary the year after I had gone to the field. In 1955 her parents asked her to accompany them back to their birthplace in Sweden. She was moved by the Lord, however, not to quit her job at our church or to accompany them, so she was at the church, where I first met her on the day in Dayton when I began my furlough. I immediately had the deep conviction that the Holy Spirit was leading us together and that we would spend our lives serving the Lord in the Far East. Eight months later, on November 1, 1958, we were married in our home church. We were able to go to the Philippines together in the midsummer of 1959. Again my work was concentrated in the seminary, both in teaching and in leadership. Two of our children were born during that term of service.

In 1963 we again went back to the United States on furlough. On the way home, we stopped in Hong Kong for preaching and fellowship with the missionaries there. In November of that year, we were surprised to receive word that the missionaries in Hong Kong had sent us an invitation to come there for fifteen months to take the place of other missionaries leaving on furlough. Though at the time we wanted to return to the Philippines to continue our ministry and knew that work in Hong Kong would involve a completely different culture and language, we still felt led by the Holy Spirit to accept this invitation.

During those fifteen months, beginning in June of 1964, as a pastor of Calvary Baptist Church in Hong Kong, we began to study the difficult Cantonese language with another couple.

As much as we loved the Filipino people and the work there, we had a clear leading of the Holy Spirit about staying in Hong Kong permanently, so we immediately asked for permission to transfer fields and were assigned by the mission to Hong Kong. This began a ministry of thirty years and the later opening of the ministry into mainland China.

Soon we were using the language to teach and preach, and within several years we began teaching in a newly opened Bible school, which was founded by our mission. We also helped several different established churches and directed an evangelistic medical clinic. For six years I was also the president of the Bible school.

In the fall of 1979 China was just opening to tourists after many years of being completely closed to any outsiders. I was asked to go on a tour to three major cities with a group of seven leaders, including the president of our mission. I remember how we would fill our suitcases with Bibles and booklets of every shape and description so that we could witness on the streets to English-speaking university students. Our bold witness might have seemed foolish to some, but I can remember that the Holy Spirit gave us courage not to be afraid of witnessing in that very dangerous situation. The following year I led a group of fourteen Bible college students and their professors from the United States back to those same three cities in China. The Lord blessed with many witnessing opportunities and several people accepted the Lord.

In the fall of 1983 a missionary colleague who had, for more than a year, been going at regular intervals to a large city in China to witness to university students urged me to pray about doing the same thing. There were many tens of thousands of university students in Shanghai, and he felt that two of us could independently and safely work there. After much prayer, the Holy Spirit laid this on my heart as a clear leading of the Lord.

Beginning that fall, I went to that city for this ministry five times each year during the vacations and semester breaks in the Bible school schedule. I would stay for ten days at a time. At first, I had to go into the parks of the city to get the contacts for witness. As the number of those being dealt with increased, however, I would simply contact the ones I had seen before by letter, and they would bring their friends to my room to hear the gospel.

In that godless Communist atmosphere, I knew that I could depend on the Holy Spirit to go ahead of me and prepare the hearts of the ones I would be dealing with. I knew also that He would put a wall of protection around me so that I would be unhindered and that He would continue to work in hearts after I returned to Hong Kong.

Many began to respond to the gospel and accept Christ as Savior. My work was not only to help them come to the Lord but also to disciple them so that they would grow and become productive followers of the Lord. Then, the Holy Spirit also opened the opportunity to meet many house/family church leaders in the area. Because their churches were forbidden and had to meet in secret, I dared not work with them in the places where they met. Rather, they would come to my room in ones and twos, study the Bible with me, and then go back to their small churches to teach these same truths to their brothers and sisters in the Lord.

In late 1993, after forty-one years as active missionaries in the Philippines, Hong Kong, and China, we came back to the United States to retire. The Lord continued to open the door for us to go back to the Far East about five months each year, with our main focus on continuing the five three-to-four week trips to China. (In August 2000, four policemen questioned Carson in his hotel room and then escorted him to a plane and told him not to return until he had an invitation and permission from the univerity and the authorities.) We are trusting the Lord, through the ministry of the Holy Spirit, to continue to work and move in the hearts of the ones we deal with in each place and to bring eternal fruit from those labors.

"According to my earnest expectation and my hope, that in nothing I shall be ashamed, but that with all boldness, as always, so now also Christ shall be magnified in my body, whether it be by life, or by death. For me to live is Christ, and to die is gain" (Philippians 1:20-21).

*The Holy Spirit's Ministry in the Life of a Teacher: Walter Gilbert Fremont Jr. (July 20, 1924)*

I remember that as a six-year-old child, I stood in our yard in Florida, looked up at the beautiful clouds, and said, "God, I believe in you and want to know you." I then asked Mother about joining the church. The pastor came and talked to me about baptism and what it meant to join the church. I joined the church a week after I was baptized.

In the third grade I heard the gospel explained by an assistant Methodist pastor who was taking us on a "Friendly Indian" fossil hunting trip. When I was twelve years old, one of my paper customers, Charlie Hautt, witnessed to me and explained the gospel again. I thought I was already saved because I had been baptized and had joined the church. I was morally good because I was a Boy Scout and tried to live by the Scout laws. When I was sixteen years old my buddy, Bob Brown, who was a fellow junior assistant Scoutmaster, witnessed to me several times. Then, after a New Year's Day Bible club retreat, he witnessed to me again. I resented his testimony because I considered myself a Christian. Three days later, on January 4, 1941, he and a friend cornered me after a Scout meeting, and I accepted Christ as my Savior. He invited me to a weekly Bible study for teens and college and career people and he encouraged me to be involved in his tract ministry. We put a tract through the ventilation slit in every locker of our five-hundred-student high school. During the following summer I worked on a camp staff as a bugler, canoe instructor, and lifeguard of a regional Scout camp at Pike Lake near Bainbridge, Ohio. Being the only

Christian on the staff, I decided to drop a hundred cellophane-wrapped tracts (gospel bombs) all over the camp. That caused quite a stir, and they never found out who bombed the camp.

As a born-again Christian I experienced the joy of the Lord overflowing in praise, thanksgiving, and worship because of my salvation and the indwelling Holy Spirit. I often went up to a place in Kettering, Ohio, in front of the Patterson monument overlooking the countryside and the golf course where no one could overhear me thanking and praising the Lord. On the first Easter morning after I accepted Christ, I remember speeding down the half-mile Schantz Avenue hill on my bicycle after finishing my paper route at 6:30, shouting praises to God for His resurrection. I regularly have times and find special places to praise the Lord where I am not disturbed by the pressures of things or people around me. I am still thrilled and enjoy experiencing God's revelation of Himself in His Word and through His creation. The following are some of my most memorable times of praise, thanksgiving, and rejoicing:

Viewing God's majestic power in the midst of a mid-Atlantic winter storm with sixty-foot waves hitting the top of the three smokestacks on the ocean liner carrying troops to Europe and seeing the effects of a hurricane in Charleston, South Carolina, and a typhoon in Hong Kong.

Experiencing God's unlimited creativeness on a 150-mile ferryboat ride through fjords between Flam and Bergen, Norway, and hiking in the Grand Canyon and the Alps, and climbing Diamond Head on Oahu, Hawaii.

Getting a glimpse of God's ultimate holiness as the Holy Spirit gave protection and victory over the lusts of the flesh and allowed me to enter marriage chaste and pure.

Bowing to and trusting in God's complete control in bringing me through dangerous and difficult situations unharmed in Europe during World War II.

Recognizing God's infinite wisdom in allowing me to have amyotrophic lateral sclerosis and, through that disease, completely changing and expanding my ministry.

Resting in God's perfect love in salvation and being called to declare and to share it with others in a teaching, camping, writing, and soulwinning ministry.

Through high school frugality was my distinguishing characteristic, for my father ingrained within us boys the work ethic and the necessity of saving at least 20 percent of every dollar for investment. My goal to be a millionaire strongly directed my energies. My career plan did not include college, for I was going into toolmaking and tool design. After high school graduation in 1942 I began an apprenticeship in toolmaking at the National Cash Register Company. That summer, in a Bible conference at the Chautaqua grounds south of Miamisburg, Ohio, my brother and I dedicated our lives to full-time Christian ministry, and I was aware of being filled with (controlled by) the Holy Spirit. My sin of covetousness with its materialistic goals and selfish desires disappeared and was replaced with a persistent love for lost souls and a spirit of contentment, thankfulness, and giving (I Timothy 6:6-10). I remember that all of us who made a decision that Wednesday night walked around the conference grounds passing out tracts and witnessing. From then on I knew that the Lord was going to use me in some type of ministry. I witnessed at work and invited people to the Bible study.

I was drafted into the army the following March 1943 and was able to lead my first soul to Christ in basic training at Camp Davis, North Carolina. I knew I would have to have some college training to be prepared to serve the Lord in a teaching or preaching ministry, so I applied for the Army Specialized Training Program and was sent to Carnegie Tech (now Carnegie-Mellon University) for mechanical engineering training. After a year I was sent back to the regular army because the program was phased out. As a sergeant I did a lot of teaching to the new recruits. I then knew that the Holy Spirit had empowered me with the gift of teaching that I had developed in the Boy Scouts teaching scouting skills. When overseas in Europe, I heard about the GI bill and knew that God had provided a way for me to go to college to study to be a teacher.

After being discharged in March 1946, I applied to several Christian schools. They did not take me because they were full, so I enrolled in the city university (University of Dayton). My wife and I graduated three years later. I had married two years previously to a young RN and we became a gospel team (the Holy Spirit, my wife, and I), dedicated to full-time service. In 1947 I took a correspondence course in philosophy of Christian education from Mark Fakkama and became convinced that the only way I could serve the Lord in teaching was to teach in a Christian school. When I graduated with a master's degree from the University of Wisconsin, I applied to a number of Christian schools, but they were leery of me because I did not have any Bible training. The Holy Spirit led me to take a year of Bible at Bob Jones University. When I arrived, the vice president asked me to teach while taking a year of Bible courses. The next year I became a full-time faculty member. Two years later I assumed the position as dean of the School of Education. I continued to teach ten or more hours in education and psychology while pursuing my doctorate from Penn State University. We can expect the guidance and gifts of the Holy Spirit at salvation and the fruit of the Holy Spirit and the empowering of the gifts following dedication, but the convicting power of the Holy Spirit can come at any time. Jesus compared the Holy Spirit to the wind (John 3:8). The wind of God's Spirit and the wind of God's creation are very similar. They both have their ways, times, and seasons. Sometimes the wind of the Holy Spirit is like the stirrings of a gentle breeze and we are refreshed; sometimes it is like the power of a hurricane and we are awed. However, the convicting power of the Holy Spirit will always be bound up with the Word. The Holy Spirit always points away from Himself to Christ, with the eternal goal of building the body of Christ, the church.

I have seen the convicting power of the Spirit manifested many times during the course of my ministry. One time it was at an evangelistic meeting in a small church. The evangelist, Glen Schunk, was a powerful preacher of soulwinning, and in about every third sentence he quoted a Scripture verse from memory. On the fourth night of this meeting almost everyone responded to the invitation. During the next two months, after the meeting, the size of the congregation doubled so that we had to enlarge the auditorium. In my classroom ministry at the university, I did not see such dramatic manifestations of the Holy Spirit; however, I went out every other weekend speaking in camps and family seminars. I also taught Sunday school to teenagers and to adults. Because of my experience in camping with the Boy Scouts and in the army, I was convinced that camping was the ideal way to reach teens and adults. Without life's normal distractions they could view and experience God's unlimited creation and hear the Word preached at least three times a day.

In the 1950s I directed a Young Life Club and took the young people camping at the five-hundred-acre Awanita Valley Camp in the mountains near Greenville, South Carolina. One of these camps seemed a disaster because only twenty-seven attended and it rained the whole weekend. We showed a gospel film, preached seven messages, sang every song, put on every skit, and played every indoor game we knew. There were only two salvation decisions that weekend, but the next Monday night three girls met me before club meeting crying and under conviction to accept the Lord. Over the next three weeks a revival hit the high school with over forty decisions for Christ. One decision was made in the middle of a home economics class and another on the football players' bus returning from a game.

Every summer during the 1960s I directed a two-week camp at the Proud Lake Campground near Wixsom, Michigan, for five Baptist churches. My duties included being the bugler, lifeguard, boy's dorm supervisor, and teacher for two morning Bible classes. My wife, Trudy, served as the nurse and cook. We had a visiting evangelist for the evening services. One of the pastors brought his whole ball team of Detroit hoods that he was trying to reach with the gospel. They gave us problems the whole week until Thursday. One by one, throughout the day, all of them broke down crying, begging to be saved. Other campers, during the song service and message, would go outside crying and making decisions with their counselors. After the campfire service, I was making "rounds" to be sure that everybody was in the dorm. I found five boys around the campfire burning a pair of tennis shoes. I asked them about it, and one of them answered, "We were discussing how we can make things right with people at home from whom we had stolen things. Since I did not know who the person was that I'd stolen them from, I decided to burn them because I can't wear stolen shoes since I'm a Christian."

In the 1970s I held a weekend camp for four Baptist pastors at a rented state park campground near Raleigh, North Carolina. I took along a graduate ministerial student as the song leader. I preached four sermons and showed a gospel film, and the song leader preached the final sermon. When he gave the invitation, most of the 150 teenagers made a decision. Several of the pastors said that a revival continued in their churches over a number of weeks, affecting not only teens but also the adults.

In the 1970s and 1980s I was heavily involved in holding family seminars at the Wilds Christian Camp. I remember many times when the convicting power of the Holy Spirit was evident and four of us counseled till 2 A.M., with people getting saved, dedicating their lives, and confessing all manner of sins.

The prerequisite for all of these out-pourings of the Holy Spirit's convicting power was the Word of God strongly preached, with an emphasis always on Christ's atonement for man's sin, accompanied by fervent prayer that the Holy Spirit would convict sinners and saints and use the proclaimed Word to glorify Christ. The evident results of a genuine Holy Spirit revival are the peaceable fruit of righteousness and a desire for holiness.

I served as dean of the School of Education at BJU for thirty-seven years and taught for forty-one years until the Holy Spirit changed my ministry in 1991. Immobility and the loss of speech caused by ALS redirected my ministry to writing articles and books and praying. The only retirement for the dedicated Christian is to retire to heaven by the Rapture or death with immediate ascension of the soul. "But none of these things move me, neither count I my life dear unto myself, so that I might finish my course with joy, and the ministry, which I have received of the Lord Jesus, to testify the gospel of the grace of God" (Acts 20:24).

### *Epilogue*

Early in 2000, Darlene went to be with the Lord after faithfully serving with Carson for 41 years. In May of 2002, Joyce, a veteran former missionary to the Philippines and a widow of several years, and Carson were married and serve together in the Far East. Since their marriage they have ministered each year in Hong Kong, the Philippines, and in Guam. Joyce has a teaching ministry and both have opportunities to counsel where they minster. Three of Carson's children serve as missionaries in Hong Kong, in Guam, and in Germany. All seven children of Carson's and Walt's are serving the Lord.

Walter went to be with the Lord in January 2007 after 20 years with ALS (Amyotrophic Lateral Sclerosis). Until his death he had a positive faith attitude, daily praising his Lord for His goodness. His wife, Trudy, served with him for sixty years.

Both men fully realized the vital contribution the Spirit-filled wives made to the gospel ministry and they deserve credit and honor. The wives have reflected Christ likeness and manifested the fruit of the spirit in their lives.

## Appendix B

# GOD'S WAY TO HEAVEN

JESUS SAID, "I am the way, the truth, and the life: no man cometh unto the Father, but by me" (John 14:6). "Ye shall die in your sins: for if ye believe not that I am he, ye shall die in your sins" (John 8:24). "Whosoever committeth sin is the servant of sin" (John 8:34). "If the Son therefore shall make you free, ye shall be free indeed" (John 8:36).

"For the wages of sin is death; but the gift of God is eternal life through Jesus Christ our Lord" (Romans 6:23).

"But God commendeth his love toward us, in that, while we were yet sinners, Christ died for us. Much more then, being now justified by His blood, we shall be saved from wrath through Him" (Romans 5:8-9).

"For by grace are ye saved through faith; and that not of yourselves; it is the gift of God: not of works, lest any man should boast" (Ephesians 2:8-9).

JESUS SAID, "Except a man be born again, he cannot see the kingdom of God" (John 3:3). "For God so loved the world, that he gave his only begotten Son, that whosoever believeth in him should not perish, but have everlasting life" (John 3:16). "For God sent not his Son into the world to condemn the world; but that the world through him might be saved" (John 3:17).

"Repent therefore, and be converted, that your sins may be blotted out" (Acts 3:19).

"That if thou shalt confess with thy mouth the Lord Jesus, and shalt believe in thine heart that God hath raised him from the dead, thou shalt be saved. For with the heart man believeth unto righteousness; and with the mouth confession is made unto salvation. For whosoever shall call upon the name of the Lord shall be saved" (Romans 10:9-10, 13).

"But as many as received him, to them gave he power to become the sons of God, even to them that believe on his name" (John 1:12).

"And this is the record, that God hath given to us eternal life, and this life is in his Son. He that hath the Son hath life; and he that hath not the Son of God hath not life. These things have I written unto you that believe on the name of the Son of God; that ye may know that ye have eternal life, and that ye may believe on the name of the Son of God" (I John 5:11-13).

"Therefore being justified by faith, we have peace with God through our Lord Jesus Christ" (Romans 5:1).

"There is therefore now no condemnation to them which are in Christ Jesus, who walk not after the flesh, but after the Spirit" (Romans 8:1).

JESUS SAID, "Go ye into all the world, and preach the gospel to every creature. He that believeth and is baptized shall be saved; but he that believeth not shall be damned" (Mark 16:15-16).

# GOD'S COMMANDMENTS

JESUS SAID, "Thou shalt love the Lord thy God with all thy heart, and with all thy soul, and with all thy mind" (Matthew 22:37).

1. "Thou shalt have no other gods before me" (Exodus 20:3).
2. "Thou shalt not make unto thee any graven image" (Exodus 20:4).
3. "Thou shalt not take the name of the Lord thy God in vain" (Exodus 20:7).
4. "Remember the sabbath day, to keep it holy" (Exodus 20:8).

JESUS SAID, "Thou shalt love thy neighbor as thyself" (Matthew 22:39).

1. "Honor thy father and thy mother: that thy days may be long upon the land" (Exodus 20:12).
2. "Thou shalt not kill" (Exodus 20:13).
3. "Thou shalt not commit adultery" (Exodus 20:14).
4. "Thou shalt not steal" (Exodus 20:15).
5. "Thou shalt not bear false witness against thy neighbor" (Exodus 20:16).
6. "Thou shalt not covet" (Exodus 20:17).

JESUS SAID, "If ye love me, keep my commandments" (John 14:15).

# SCRIPTURE INDEX